Mary Magdalene –
Beyond the Myth

Esther de Boer

SCM PRESS LTD

Translated by John Bowden from the Dutch *Maria Magdalena: De mythe voorbij; Op zoek naar wie zij werkelijk is,* published 1996 by Meinema, Zoetermeer.

© Meinema 1996

Translation © John Bowden 1997

0 334 02690 3

First published 1997 by
SCM Press Ltd
9–17 St Albans Place London NI ONX

Typeset at The Spartan Press Ltd,
Lymington, Hants
Printed in Great Britain by
Biddles Ltd, Guildford and King's Lynn

To the memory of
Geertje Streefland, Esther Ras and Maartje Visser,
my mother and my grandmothers,
to whom I am greatly indebted.

Contents

Foreword

Mary Magdalene must have had much to tell. She had followed Jesus of Nazareth, the Christ of Christian faith, from the beginning of his work. She was one of the few of his followers to be present at his crucifixion and burial. She was the first to proclaim the resurrection. Nevertheless Mary Magdalene has become known above all as the incarnation of feminine attractiveness.

In this book, I shall show how this image was not developed until the fifth and sixth centuries and circulated only in the Western tradition of the church. I hope to involve readers in a quest for what the first four centuries tell us about Mary Magdalene.

I want to thank all those who have helped me in writing the book. Their help has ranged from expressions of interest to critical comments on the text. In every form, it has been indispensable.

I am particularly grateful to the Dutch Reformed Church of Ouderkerk aan de Amstel, which made it possible for this book actually to appear. The church members supported me as their minister so that I could devote three months to the quest for Mary Magdalene. I much appreciate that.

What follows is meant for anyone who is interested in Mary Magdalene for whatever reason. It has been written out of a desire to learn more about the significance of Jesus in a new way, by means of Mary Magdalene.

Ouderkerk aan de Amstel, June 1996   Esther A.de Boer

June 1993. To Vézelay in France for the third time, the mediaeval pilgrimage place of Mary Magdalene. From the depths of the valley look up at the town on its high hill. Climb up to the basilica as the pilgrims used to do. Weary, longing. Like them, enter and become captivated with the gloom of the impressive narthex. Look up, see Christ, and by him be personally invited to go further inside. From the gloom into the light. One is drawn along by the surprising play of light, through the lofty nave. One knows that one is being welcomed, and is not just on one's own way.

And then, just before one reaches the light, the descent into the crypt. It is dark there. Like a cave. Candle-light flickers over what may have been Mary Magdalene. Silence, death. 'Lord, just let me remain here.' But get up, climb again. Blinking in the light, going to stand before the light, before the altar and there to find on the lectern:

Blessed Mary Magdalene,
you who were redeemed from seven demons,
pray Jesus the Lord for us, that he may free us
from what holds us in chains, far from him,
the source of love and forgiveness.
You who chose the best part
by listening to the word of God,
pray Jesus the Lord for us
that his word may free us from lies and darkness.
You who were chosen to be the first witness
of Jesus Christ, freed from the chains of death,
pray Jesus the Lord for us that we may live in abundance
through the fellowship
of the Father, the Son and the Holy Spirit.

I

Beyond the Myth

Some years ago, when I was studying theology at the Free University of Amsterdam, I made a discovery which has come to mean a good deal to me. At that time I was trying to reconcile myself with a tradition of faith in which men's names kept cropping up: Abraham, Moses, David, Isaiah, Peter, Paul, Augustine, Anselm, Luther, Calvin – whereas there did not seem to be many women. The women's group in our faculty claimed that our study gave a one-sided picture and therefore had prepared an extra reading list for each examination, but in the end that was no more than rummaging on the periphery. Or was it more?

The bibliography for the examination that I wanted to take in the summer of 1982 contained Elaine Pagels' book *The Gnostic Gospels*. In it she describes the origin of the early church tradition, on the basis of writings which were found in 1945 near Nag Hammadi in Egypt. In the introduction she relates: 'In 1896 a German Egyptologist . . . bought in Cairo a manuscript that, to his amazement, contained the Gospel of Mary (Magdalene).'[1]

A Gospel of Mary? I knew that in the Bible the Gospels are attributed to Matthew, Mark, Luke and John. And I knew that there were other Gospels outside the Bible. However, they had names like Peter, Thomas, James, Philip and Judas. I became so fascinated that this began to determine the direction of my studies. I wanted to read the Gospel of Mary in the original language. I wanted to be able to understand it and place it. First I was simply interested in the Gospel of Mary itself, but later I also became interested in the figure of Mary Magdalene. I proved to be not the only one who was aware of the existence of the Gospel. *The Gnostic Gospels* had been translated into Dutch in 1980 and became something of a best-seller. There were articles about it and study weekends devoted to it. It was making quite a mark, not only on me but on others. Mary Magdalene had so far meant nothing to me. She played her part at Easter as a kind of extra, but that was all. However, down the centuries an image of her seemed to have come into being which had inspired many people: to repent; to be converted; to embark on a mystical way to God; to write poems, plays and novels; to paint pictures; and to be socially concerned. In the study weekends we discovered that in the course of history Mary Magdalene enjoyed great popularity, but that the interest was more in her sexuality than in her testimony.

Nevertheless Mary Magdalene must have had much to tell. She had followed Jesus from the beginning of his work. She was one of the few who were present at the crucifixion and the burial. She was the first to proclaim the resurrection.

However, Mary Magdalene has gone down in history above all as an attractive and very sinful woman, who thanks to Jesus was converted and repented. This portrait led a number of people to write about her: Victor Saxer, Marjorie Malvern and Susan Haskins did pioneering work here.[2] So far, though, little attention has been paid to the earliest traditions about Mary Magdalene. But since they are such important testimony, it is worth while setting out carefully what can be discovered about her in antiquity. That is my aim in this book.[3] It is a quest for who Mary Magdalene might really have been. It is a quest for her story.

The New Testament Gospels are the earliest sources to mention Mary Magdalene. She also appears in the writings of the church fathers. Over the past two centuries, yet other texts have been discovered, which were not incorporated into the church's tradition, but which shed light on Mary Magdalene. The Gospel of Mary is one of them.

Before we begin the quest into antiquity, we need also to take account of the picture of Mary Magdalene which has arisen in the course of time, especially the picture that was current in the Middle Ages. This was the picture of the sister of Martha and Lazarus, the fallen woman, the sinner, who through Jesus could raise herself up again and who did penance all her life. This picture still has an influence today. It is important for us to free ourselves from it if we want to be able to read the texts from antiquity with as little prejudice as possible.

Mary Magdalene: penitent

In the Middle Ages Mary Magdalene stood in high esteem, to such a degree that she rivalled Mary the mother of Jesus in popularity.[4]

After Jerusalem, Rome and Santiago de Compostela, the city of Vézelay in France was the most important place of pilgrimage in Christendom. The basilica of Vézelay, a splendid romanesque building, houses relics of Mary Magdalene. For centuries they attracted many pilgrims.[5]

Even now the basilica is a great draw. No longer so much because of its relics, but above all because of the special play of light and shade which is so amazing. The narthex of the church is gloomy. Light streams around the altar. Moreover at the solstice in June the light falls in such a way that you can get the feeling of walking out of the gloom towards the light, almost in the footsteps of the Risen Christ. Then in the aisle the light is concentrated in regular patches, like so many stones by which you can cross the river of death.

There is now a statue of Mary Magdalene in the church. That was not the case in the Middle Ages. Mary Magdalene was to be found high above the entrance on the outside of the basilica. Statues were not needed in the building. The play of light drew the pilgrims into her story, the dark story that through Jesus could become a story of light, the story of Mary Magdalene the penitent.

Before Mary Magdalene, the sister of Martha and Lazarus, was converted, she led a far from pious life. She sat very loose to morality. She is said to have been a prostitute. The seven deadly sins had her in their grip: pride, avarice, gluttony, lust, laziness, jealousy and anger. How did that come about? According to some stories she was corrupted by her wealth and beauty. According to others she was the bride at the marriage at Cana. Her bridegroom, John, was so impressed by the miracle that Jesus did there, turning water into wine, that he abandoned his new wife in order to follow Jesus. Bitterly disappointed, Mary left for the city of Jerusalem, and there went from bad to worse.

But Jesus changed that. Finally she gave up her worldly life. In public she knelt before him, washed his feet with her tears of repentance and anointed him with fragrant oil. From that moment she supported him wherever she could. She became a devoted follower and could also give financial support to Jesus and his disciples.

When the twelve disciples left Jesus in the lurch, she remained faithful to him. Her zeal was rewarded on Easter morning. She was allowed to be the first witness of the resurrection. She was able to escape the subsequent persecution of Christians and went to France, to which she brought the gospel. She spent the last years of her life in a cave, where she devoted herself wholly to Christ. Angels brought her food and finally accompanied her to heaven.

Significance

Mary Magdalene is depicted in a thirteenth-century Italian painting as she was imagined as a recluse: her nakedness covered by her long hair. Eight cameos in the background relate her life story. In the foreground Mary Magdalene is making a sign of blessing with one hand. With the other, she displays an open scroll. On it stand the words

> *Ne desperetis vos qui peccare soletis exemploque meo vos reparate Deo.*
>
> (Do not despair, you who are prone to sin, but by my example restore your relationship with God.)[6]

That was the significance of St Mary Magdalene. She embodied a call to conversion. Her life story showed believers that there is grace with God, however far they had departed from him. Repentance and zeal could bring them from the lowest depths to the greatest heights.

Not only the penitence and zeal of Mary Magdalene but also her devotion and dedication have gone down as models in history. From her conversion onwards she is said to have drunk in Jesus' words without attaching much importance to everyday needs. Thus she chose the good part, as Jesus emphasized by comparing her with her sister, who drew his attention to Mary's duties as a woman. 'It shall not be taken from her.' Even when Jesus has been crucified and buried, she does not let him go. Her later fasting and prayer complete the picture: Mary Magdalene stands for a life of contemplation and asceticism. She symbolizes the way to become one with Christ. She is the bride alongside the bridegroom.

Mary Magdalene meant much to Margery Kempe in the fifteenth century and to Catherine of Siena in the fourteenth. The former is known as a mystic: the descriptions of her visions have been preserved. The latter, respected for her ascetical life-style, could stand beside kings and popes with her wisdom and piety. Both women were able to defend their 'unfeminine' choice with Mary Magdalene as a model. They sought the same complete devotion and dedication to the Lord.[7]

Liturgy

The festival of St Mary Magdalene is on 22 July. That is the day appointed in the calendar of saints for her commemoration.

Anyone who opens a Roman Missal from before the Second Vatican Council and looks up the mass dedicated to her, will first see beside her name the word 'penitent'. This designation is brought out in the Gospel reading for the day. It is taken from the Gospel of Luke, in which a woman who is generally known as a sinner washes Jesus' feet with her tears, kisses them, and anoints them with precious myrrh (Luke 7.36–50). This gesture is interpreted as penance for her many sins.

The other reading is from the Song of Songs (3.2–5; 8.6–7). This describes the quest for the true beloved:

I will rise now and go about the city, in the streets and in the squares;
I will seek him whom my soul loves (3.2).

The woman sets out on her search in the middle of the night. She

persists in it, despite discouragement from the watchmen of the
city. When she has found him, she says:

> Set me as a seal upon your heart, as a seal upon your arm;
> for love is as strong as death (8.6).

The reading also contains a clear warning:

> I adjure you, daughters of Jerusalem . . . that you stir not up
> nor awaken love until it pleases (3.5).

Thus after penitence and regret, the true loving zeal of Mary
Magdalene is emphasized. In the silent prayer of the priest at the
offertory the two come together and her penitence is called her
'generous service of love'.

The Psalm text at the introit to the mass calls those blessed who
are blameless according to the law of the Lord (Ps.119.1). The
Psalm texts at the offertory and the communion celebrate the
justice of the king and the splendour of the queen, with whom
Mary Magdalene is identified (Ps.45.10; 119.121–2, 128).

And the Psalm text before the Gospel runs:

> You love righteousness and hate wickedness. Therefore God,
> your God, has anointed you with the oil of gladness (Ps.45.8).

By 'your God' the Missal means Jesus. The anointing by the
woman who was a sinner, Mary Magdalene, is thus interpreted as
an act of God himself.

As a conclusion to the mass there follows the prayer:

> May we . . . through the intercession of Blessed Mary
> Magdalene be freed from all evil.[8]

Blessed Mary Magdalene: on her festival she is celebrated as
the penitent. She is a notorious sinner who learns to know true
love, a splendid queen alongside the king of justice. Apart from
Mary the mother of Jesus, Magdalene is the only woman saint
who has the creed in her mass. That is because her mission on
Easter morning has an apostolic character. She is seen as an
apostle before the apostles.[9]

Art

Down the ages Mary Magdalene has been a favourite subject for artists. Her story makes her a colourful and dramatic figure. Eroticism, tragedy and power can be brought together in this one person, so close to Christ.

In pictorial art Mary Magdalene can usually be recognized by the jar of ointment which she is carrying. A Bible, a skull and a crucifix can often be found in her immediate surroundings. Sometimes one sees her depicted as a young, lascivious girl looking up to heaven, and sometimes as an emaciated and ravaged woman. Her clothing may be rich, or she may have only her long hair to cover her body. Popular themes from her life are her sinful existence, the anointing of Jesus' feet, her presence at the crucifixion, the encounter with the risen Lord, her later monastic existence and her welcome into heaven.

The same themes appear in literature, but in a much fuller way. Thus writers are fond of looking more closely at the relationship between Jesus and Mary Magdalene. For example Jacobus de Voragine (thirteenth century) writes in his collection *The Golden Legend*:

> He drove seven evil spirits out of her and made her glow right through with his love. He made her his special friend and had her as his host and his steward when they were travelling . . . If he saw her weeping, he wept too. Our of love for her he raised her brother Lazarus from the dead and healed her sister Martha of issues of blood which she had had for seven years.[10]

Two contemporary examples are the books by Luise Rinser and Nikos Kazantzakis. The latter portrays Mary Magdalene as a sexual threat to Jesus' calling. The former depicts her as a critical woman in search of the truth in life, who here finds Jesus as a guide.[11]

Social work

In this way Mary Magdalene has left traces in religious instruction, in mysticism, in liturgy, in pictorial art and literature. But that is not all. She can also be found in social life. In the Middle

Ages she was the patron saint of those who tended vineyards, gardeners, apothecaries, glove-makers, perfume manufacturers, hatters, weavers, seafarers, prisoners and later of gypsies. But above all, her life-story has remained a motive force behind care for prostitutes and those who because of their weak social position could succumb to prostitution.

This care was already practised in the Middle Ages by the order of the Penitents of St Mary Magdalene. The order was formed to work towards the conversion of women and girls in moral danger. The convents of this order devoted themselves to teaching.

All over Europe in the eighteenth and nineteenth centuries, houses, convents and institutions came into being which were given the name of Mary Magdalene. They were meant for the improvement of the lot of the many women who saw no other opportunity to make their living than prostitution. A modern example is 'The Magdalene Centre' in Seoul, South Korea, which is helping many thousands of girls who work in in the sex tourism industry to build a new existence.[12]

Nowadays Mary Magdalene is increasingly seen as a woman friend of Jesus.

It is worth noting that the Philothea Foundation, for women who have or have had a relationship with a priest, has recently changed its name to the Magdala Foundation.[13] Philothea means friend of God.

The picture in fragments

Mary Magdalene, the fallen woman who through Jesus was able to rise again, the sister of Martha and Lazarus, the sinner who anointed Jesus' feet. That is the image that has come to dominate the Western tradition of the church.

However, it is no more than an image. It is an image which individuals have capably challenged in the course of history, but it nevertheless remains. Only in this century has it really begun to fall to pieces.

When the calendar of saints was revised in connection with the Second Vatican Council (1969), it was said of Mary Magdalene that her day celebrates only the one to whom Christ appeared after the resurrection and in no sense the sister of St Martha, or the woman who was a sinner and whose sins the Lord forgave.[14]

As we look at the fragments of what once was St Mary Magdalene, penitent, questions arise.
Mary Magdalene: not the converted sinner?
Not the Mary who drank in Jesus' words, in contrast to her busy sister Martha?
How did this misleading picture arise?
And in that case, who was Mary Magdalene?

The portrait discredited

In the course of history the image of Mary Magdalene has time and again been criticized by those engaged in studying the biblical details. In 1517 there was Jacques Lefèvre d'Étaples. At that time this Protestant humanist published his book *De Maria Magdalena et triduo Christi disceptatione* (On Mary Magdalene and the Departure of Christ After Three Days), in answer to questions from a former pupil. In it he defended the view that the woman who was a sinner, the sister of Martha, and Mary Magdalene were three distinct biblical figures. In 1521 he was condemned. The theological faculty of Paris stated that Lefèvre's teaching must be regarded as dangerous.[15] But his thesis found an echo.

In 1773 the Benedictine exegete and historian Dom Augustine Calmet wrote his *Dissertation on the Three Marys*. In the same century the need arose also to have a liturgical celebration of the biblical Mary Magdalene. There was a wish to reserve the feast of 22 July exclusively for Mary Magdalene and to venerate Mary, the sister of Martha, on another date. This reform did not meet with official approval.[16]

It was Peter Ketter in 1935 who stood up for the biblical Mary Magdalene. In his book *The Magdalene Question* he showed that the imagery which had formed around Mary Magdalene does an injustice to the biblical details about her.[17]

This view is now shared by many people, and since the Second Vatican Council it has also got as far as influencing the official calendar of saints.

Discussion

All this does not mean that the picture of Mary Magdalene which came into being did not rest on biblical details. The discussion which kept breaking out turned on the question which biblical details these were.

The name Mary occurs on different occasions in the New Testament. To indicate which Mary this is, she is often denoted more precisely: for example as Mary the mother of James and Joseph, Mary of Clopas, Mary the sister of Martha, Mary of Magdala. Despite these more precise indications, it is not always easy to distinguish the different Marys. What are we to think of Mary the mother of James the Younger and Joses, Mary of Joses and Mary of James (Mark 15.20,47; 16.1)? Is she one and the same person?

Mary of Magdala is sometimes named along with various other Marys and therefore cannot be identified with them. However, her name is never mentioned in the same breath as that of Martha's sister. That means that *a priori* the possibility must not be ruled out that Mary of Magdala and Mary the sister of Martha could be one and the same person. Care is needed.

In addition, in many New Testament stories in which women play a major role, their names are not given. Thus anyone in search of the identity of a named woman can possibly also appeal to these stories.

The story of Mary Magdalene the penitent is based on a combination of the following biblical details.

The Gospel of John describes Mary the sister of Martha with the words:

> Who had anointed the Lord with ointment and wiped his feet with her hair (John 11.2).[18]

In Luke it is a 'woman of the city, who was a sinner' who wiped Jesus' feet with her hair and anointed them (Luke 7.37).

So Martha's sister is identified with the woman who was a sinner. Soon after that Luke talks of

> Mary, called Magdalene, from whom seven evil spirits had gone out (Luke 8.2).

He reports that she and other women who had been healed went around the country with Jesus and his disciples (Luke 8.1–3). The seven evil spirits are interpreted as the sins of the woman who was a sinner in the previous story. So Mary Magdalene could become the woman who was a sinner and who anointed Jesus, and thus at the same time the sister of Martha who anointed him.

Luke's woman who was a sinner, who 'loved much' (Luke 7.47), is taken with the Samaritan woman in John 4 who had had several husbands and who proclaimed Jesus as Messiah, and also with the adulterous woman in John 8.1–11 who is saved from stoning by Jesus. 'Go and sin no more,' he tells her.

Her new state of life is then described again in Luke (10.38–42). Mary, Martha's sister, is sitting there at the feet of Jesus and listening to what he has to say. According to Jesus, by doing this, 'she has chosen the good part, and it will not be taken from her'.

John speaks of Jesus' love for Mary: 'Now Jesus loved Martha and her sister and Lazarus' (John 11.5).

The puzzling question has always been whether these biblical data are all connected with one person.

There are three weak links in the chain of biblical data and in their application to Mary Magdalene. First, the use of texts from one Gospel to answer questions raised by another. Secondly, the interpretation of the seven evil spirits as sins. And thirdly, the identification of Mary the sister of Martha who lives in Bethany, near Jerusalem, with Mary who owes her name Magdalene to the place Magdala by the Sea of Galilee.[19]

East and West

Modern exegetes leave no doubt that the biblical exegesis which has led to the story of Mary Magdalene is illegitimate.

Those who argue for the classic image which has formed round Mary Magdalene have to concede that the New Testament gives no clear pointer towards the identification of Mary Magdalene with the sister of Martha and the woman who was a sinner, who anointed Jesus' feet.

However, they would say, the early tradition does make this identification.

In 1922, Ulrich Holzmeister published an interesting investigation. He demonstrated that up to the fifth century there was no specific tradition about the identification. The church fathers either do not concern themselves with the problem or in passing begin from various possibilities: three women, two women or one woman.[20]

From the fifth century onwards, there was a shift in the church tradition. In the Eastern tradition Mary Magdalene has remained the figure that she is in the Bible: the witness to the resurrection. She is not celebrated as a 'penitent' but as 'ointment bearer' (not the ointment for anointing the feet or the head, but the ointment which was meant to anoint the dead body of Jesus) and 'like an apostle'.[21] A number of church fathers from the Eastern tradition depict her explicitly as disciple and apostle, even though she is a woman. Thus Gregory of Antioch (sixth century) in one his sermons makes Christ say to the women at the tomb:

> Proclaim to my disciples the mysteries which you have seen. Become the first teachers of the teachers. Peter, who has denied me, must learn that I can also choose women as apostles.[22]

It was the Western tradition which definitively identified Mary Magdalene with the woman who was a sinner in Luke and the sister of Martha, and made her a 'penitent'.

The name which is then mentioned is that of Gregory the Great (sixth century), the pope who is known among other things for the form of chant which bears his name, Gregorian. He was a popular preacher. For him, important themes were the Last Judgment and the call to penance. His sermons about Mary Magdalene as the penitent *par excellence* have become classics.[23]

A deliberate caricature

> Anyone who loves the biblical Mary Magdalene and compares her with the 'Christian' Mary Magdalene must get very angry. And to begin with, I must give vent to this anger here.

So wrote Elisabeth Moltmann-Wendel in 1980 at the beginning of her chapter about Mary Magdalene, in *The Women around Jesus*.[24] The passion expressed in these words can easily be seen.

In the Bible Mary Magdalene is the one who first bears witness to the resurrection. However, what characterizes the biblical Mary Magdalene has become overgrown and hidden from sight by the Western identification of Mary of Magdala with Luke's woman who was a sinner and the sister of Martha.

In the formation of the Western image Mary's supposedly sinful life has come to be emphasized: her conversion, her zeal and dedication. However, these facets are almost without exception derived from Luke's woman who was a sinner and Martha's sister. The fact that Mary Magdalene is the first to bear witness to the resurrection has been overshadowed by this.

That Christ appeared to Mary Magdalene is interpreted as a reward for her faithfulness. And that Mary Magdalene performed the role of apostle before the later apostles is seen as a sign of appreciation of her by Jesus. The resurrection plays an incidental role in the story of Mary Magdalene. Her conversion and devotion stand at the centre. The portrayal emphasizes her sexuality. Before her encounter with Jesus she was dissolute. After her encounter with him she turned her back on that kind of life. The fact that as a follower of Jesus and a witness to the resurrection she, too, had a story has also fallen into the background. The emphasis on her sexuality has suppressed her testimony.

Susan Haskins, who collected a great deal of material about Mary Magdalene which was published in 1993, writes:

> And so the transformation of Mary Magdalen was complete. From the gospel figure with her active role as herald of the New Life – the Apostle before the Apostles – she became the redeemed whore and Christiantity's model of repentance: a manageable, controllable figure, an effective weapon and instrument of propaganda against her own sex.[25]

According to Haskins, with Mary Magdalene the penitent the Western church of the Middle Ages disputed not only her sexuality but the sexuality of all women. In her, the ascetic church rejected everything to do with sexuality. Women were the embodiment of this. Haskins comes to the conclusion that the identification of Mary Magdalene with the woman who was a sinner in Luke and Martha's sister is a deliberately misleading exegesis of the Bible. The image of Mary Magdalene was deliberately adapted so that instead of being a woman who proclaimed the Easter gospel she became a woman who served as a role model for a misogynistic church.

Counter-Reformation

Moltmann-Wendel's anger is understandable and Haskins' argument is attractive. However, because modern exegesis sees no reason whatever for identifying the three women, we cannot assume that the Western mediaeval exegesis was deliberately misleading. Haskins does not mention any mediaeval writings which seem to support her claim. Thus there are certainly sermons of Gregory the Great in which he put emphasis on Mary Magdalene as a penitent, but there is no papal bull in which he applies this to the role of women in the church.

A look at the tradition of the Eastern churches also does not directly suggest a deliberate Western caricature of Mary Magdalene aimed at women. In the churches of the Eastern tradition, too, women have little or no active role. The fact that the East associates Mary Magdalene above all with the resurrection and not, as in the West, with sexuality and penitence, has evidently had no influence on it here.[26]

It is clear that in our day the biblical Mary Magdalene is deliberately being brought to the fore. Thus in Germany there is a woman's organization called 'The Mary of Magdala Group', which is pressing for equal rights for women in the church.[27] But was Mary also deliberately banished to the background in the Middle Ages because of the role of women? It is worth remembering the precise moment when Mary Magdalene officially became the penitent.

Before the Council of Trent (1545–1563) there were still calendars of saints which gave Mary Magdalene no predicate, or which celebrated her as the first witness to the resurrection of the Lord. Local customs to mark her day differed from place to place.[28] However, on the authority of the Council, liturgical books were produced which were binding on the whole Roman Catholic Church. Thus the Roman Missal appeared in 1570. In that first compulsory missal Mary Magdalene is given the epithet 'penitent'. Here the missal was not just taking up the image of Mary Magdalene which had been disseminated by Gregory the Great and others. This image also emerged from the Counter-Reformation church. Over against the Reformation with its doctrine of grace, the Counter-Reformation emphasized the doctrine of penance and merits. Here St Mary Magdalene could play an important role as a penitent and one who was favoured *par excellence*.[29]

Popularity

The Second Vatican Council (1962–1965) commissioned a revision of the Roman Missal, which came out in 1970. The Gospel reading on the feast day of Mary Magdalene in the revised edition of the Missal is John 20.1–18. The encounter of Mary Magdalene with the Risen Lord stands at the centre. The word 'penitent' is no longer used. The further explanation now given by the Missal is:

> Mary Magdalene was one of the women who followed Christ on his travels. She was present when he died and was the first to see him after his resurrection (Mark 16.9). Veneration of her spread in the Western church above all in the twelfth century.[30]

So you could say that Mary Magdalene was officially passed off as a penitent for precisely 400 years.

400 years is a long time, given that in each century a number of voices were raised in public against the image of Mary Magdalene the penitent. Was it the power of the church which caused this? Or is that too simple a reason?

Marjorie Malvern, who has studied the transformation of Mary Magdalene above all through plays, novels and films, thinks that while we may enquire about the possible purpose behind the image of Mary Magdalene the penitent, another question is more important. Mary Magdalene was popular in her role as the converted sinner.

How could Mary Magdalene have become so popular in this form? How are we to explain the fact that the converted sinner was for so long set over against the biblical figure and still is? This may no longer be officially the case in the Roman Missal, but it certainly still is in popular devotion.

Malvern comes to the conclusion that the metamorphosis of Mary Magdalene is not a caricature but is mythical. A myth comes into being whenever it becomes impossible or dangerous to speak publicly about certain social and religious ideas, though there is still a need to cultivate and preserve them. The image of Mary Magdalene contains reminiscences of goddesses of love, wisdom and fertility. Her transformation from the biblical Mary Magdalene meets the age-old desire for a female counterpart to the male deity.[31]

It is clear that the Western image which formed around Mary Magdalene raises many questions, questions which need to be dealt with and which I hope will be discussed in greater depth elsewhere. However, that is not what we shall be doing in this book. We are going in search of who Mary Magdalene herself could have been, in search of what she could have to tell us.

In search of who she really is

We shall be steeping ourselves in antiquity. We shall try to leave behind us the picture that we might have had, or might have, of Mary Magdalene, and all the sentiments which go with it. Then we can begin the quest through the texts of antiquity with as few presuppositions as possible.

We shall begin with the earliest writings which mention Mary Magdalene: the four Gospels which have found a place in the Bible. We shall look closely in the next chapter at what they have to tell us. We shall reflect on Mary's name, on the discipleship of women, on the events surrounding the cross and the tomb, and then allow each Gospel to speak for itself separately.

In Chapter 3 we shall then continue the quest through later texts. First we shall look at the texts which came to belong to the church tradition, and allow the church fathers their say. But we can consult yet more sources. During the past two centuries, above all in the Egyptian desert, discoveries have been made of ancient texts which were not preserved in the church tradition. They were deliberately rejected, or consigned to oblivion in one way or another. Since they have now been found, we find ourselves in the happy position of being able to study what the desert sand has protected from oblivion.

We shall leave the most striking text, the Gospel of Mary, for Chapter 4. A translation is given in that chapter of as much of this text as is known to us. We shall take account of what different scholars have so far said about the Gospel and investigate what may be of importance to us.

In Chapter 5 we shall round off the quest. We shall look at the bits of the jig-saw puzzle that we have found and try to put them together. In that way a new image of Mary Magdalene will come into being: beyond the myth.

2

The Earliest Sources
about Mary Magdalene

In a thousand things I saw you appear,
round a thousand corners I saw your shadow vanish,
in a thousand nights I heard your voice,
but now that I swim alone through the surf
of turbulent life between sharp rocks,
I feel all assurance slip away
and know that I am far from your Jerusalem

(Theo van Baaren)[1]

The earliest sources report one particular period of Mary Magdalene's life. They relate that she was present at the crucifixion of her teacher, the teacher whom she had followed virtually from the beginning of his public activity. They relate that she was one of the very few to witness his burial, and that she found the tomb empty on the third day and there received a revelation.

That, in a nutshell, is what the Bible tells about her.

The New Testament Gospels are the earliest sources that we can consult about Mary Magdalene. They are books from the second half of the first century. The Gospel of Mark is the earliest; then come Matthew and Luke, and finally John. They tell of Jesus of Nazareth. At the end of the twenties he went through Israel and aroused high expectations. Finally salvation from God would dawn for the much-tormented people. Jesus himself would be the long-expected saviour. However, after a few years he was found guilty of blasphemy by the Jewish authorities and nailed to the cross by the Roman forces of occupation as 'king of the Jews'.

Jesus is thought to have been born in 6 BCE and to have died in 30 CE.

The word 'gospel' means 'good news'. The four Gospels want to convince their readers that Jesus was in fact the promised saviour: in Hebrew 'Messiah', in Greek 'Christ'. His crucifixion did not put an end to this, but confirmed it. He had to die; he had foretold this. The Gospels end with accounts of events after his death. His tomb seemed empty and there were followers who told how they had seen him and spoken with him. On these occasions he had given them commands and also the power to go further in his footsteps. That is the motive of the evangelists and also their aim. They want to make it clear what those footsteps look like.

These are important things for us to note at the beginning of our quest for Mary Magdalene. The earliest sources which mention her are not about her. They are about Jesus. They are about events during his life and after his death, which have to convince readers that with Jesus a new time has dawned.

Another important statement to note is that the four evangelists each tell of Jesus in their own way. The four Gospels consist of stories handed down by word of mouth and in writing. These are stories about the passion and the resurrection, about healings, about the Law, about the last things, and about the parables which Jesus told. The evangelists worked these collections of stories into their Gospels and grouped them to form their own compositions.

Anyone who reads the Gospels one after another will be struck by the great similarity between Matthew, Mark and Luke. Scholars think that Matthew and Luke are dependent on the material that was the basis for Mark and that they both also knew another source. A comparison of Matthew and Luke with Mark, and of Matthew with Luke, can help us to bring out the distinctive features of each of the three evangelists. The Gospel of John stands out even on first reading for its own style and pattern of thought.

The evangelists do not just each tell their own story about Jesus. Where Mary Magdalene, too, is concerned, each gives his own picture.

The evangelists agree in three respects. All four call her Mary

Magdalene; they introduce her as one of Jesus' followers; and they make her play a role above all in connection with his crucifixion, burial and resurrection.

In the following sections we shall investigate these agreements, and then let each evangelist have his own say. On the basis of what these two approaches produce, we shall look at what the New Testament Gospels have to contribute to our quest for Mary Magdalene.

But first something different.

The evangelists tell us no more than this about Mary Magdalene. They give us far more information about Peter, for example, than about her. Popping up almost from nowhere, she stands in the spotlight on Easter morning and then disappears again as quickly as she appeared. Anyone in quest of Mary Magdalene must feel some disappointment at the sparse light that the earliest sources shed on her. Who Mary Magdalene was before she met Jesus, what kind of life she led, how old she was, how she came to be converted, what became of her later: the earliest sources leave us guessing.

This brings us to a first crossroads in our quest. What conclusion are we to draw from the fact that the evangelists tell us so little?

Researchers like Michael Baigent, Richard Leigh, Henry Lincoln and Margaret Starbird think that the silence about Mary Magdalene is deliberate. They speak of secret oral traditions which relate that Mary Magdalene was Jesus' wife and was expecting his child. To protect her and the fruit of her womb, it was necessary to keep quiet about her existence to the Roman occupying forces.[2]

This book will not investigate that aspect of the question. I shall be investigating what the texts from antiquity say and not occupy myself further with other traditions.[3]

Why the four evangelists say little about Mary Magdalene is a question to which the New Testament texts give us no answer. The most obvious reply would be that the evangelists thought that any further information about her was unimportant for the story of the belief in Jesus that they wanted to tell. More about this later.

Mary, with the surname 'of Magdala'

Reading through the birth or death notices in the papers one hardly ever comes across the name 'Magdalene' or 'Magdalena'. However, the names Magda and Madeleine do appear, and these are derivatives. So you could suppose that 'Magdalena' is a first name. Nothing is further from the truth. The four New Testament Gospels also never speak of Mary Magdalene, the name we are used to, but of Mary the Magdalene. The Gospel of Luke puts this even more emphatically, speaking of Mary who 'was called the Magdalene' (Luke 8.2). The addition 'the Magdalene' is intended to make it clear which Mary this is. It is the Mary who comes from Magdala.

Mary Magdalene: her name conjures up a picture of her background.

Magdala/Tarichea

The town of Magdala is not mentioned in the New Testament, at least in the text of the New Testament as we normally read it. But the New Testament has been handed down in a great many manuscripts, and in a few of them Magdala does occur, in a version of Mark (8.10) and one of Matthew (15.39). These read Magdala where the official text has Dalmanutha and Magadan respectively. These are two place names which scholars have not been able to identify more closely. If Mark and Matthew indeed meant Magdala, that is the place to which Jesus and his disciples crossed after he had fed four thousand people with seven loaves and a few fishes.

There, in the region of Magadan/Dalmanutha or Magdala, Pharisees asked him for a sign from heaven 'to tempt him' (Matt.16.1–4; Mark 8.11–13). If anything, we can only conclude from the New Testament that there were scribes in the region of Magdala and that the region could be reached by ship.

There has been a long discussion about the possible location of Magdala.[4] It becomes clear from the rabbinic literature that we have to look for Magdala in the neighbourhood of Tiberias, by the sea of Galilee.

Nowdays, north of Tiberias lies the small town of Mejdel. The name could recall Magdala. That is an assumption which fits closely with testimonies of earlier pilgrims who locate Magdala between Tiberias and Capernaum to the north.

There are reports of pilgrimages between the sixth and the seventeenth centuries. Without exception they bear witness that Magdala was equidistant between Tiberias and Tabga, a place close to Capernaum. Pilgrims talk of the house of Mary Magdalene that they could inspect and the church that the empress Helena (fourth century) had had built in her honour. Ricoldus de Monte Crucis in his travel account (1294) tells us that the church was no longer in use at the end of the thirteenth century. He writes:

> Then we arrived in Magdala . . ., the town of Mary Magdalene by the Sea of Gennesaret. We burst into tears and wept because we found a splendid church, completely intact, but being used as a stable. We then sang in this place and proclaimed the gospel of the Magdalene there.[5]

If Magdala in fact lay on the site of Mejdel, then Jesus *must* have been there. The city was on the road from Nazareth, the small village where Jesus grew up (around twenty miles from Magdala) to Capernaum, where he later went to live.

Capernaum was about six miles from Magdala. It is not unthinkable that Jesus knew the town well. At all events, it seems possible that he taught and perhaps healed people there, as the Gospel of Mark relates:

> And he went throughout all Galilee, preaching in their synagogues and casting out demons (Mark 1.39; cf. Matt.4.23 and Luke 8.1–3).

Recently it has become certain that there was also a synagogue in Magdala. Excavations were carried out in Mejdel between 1971 and 1977. Vergilio Corbo uncovered what he could there:[6] houses, streets, a bath house, a swimming bath, shops, squares. Unfortunately he could not get access to much of the terrain. But he made a remarkable discovery: a small synagogue from the Roman period, architecturally comparable to the synagogue of Massada. This small synagogue is now the earliest synagogue in Palestine to have been excavated.

From the excavation it seemed that at the end of the first century, the beginning of the second, or possibly even later, the synagogue was used as a reservoir for water. And further on the remains were found of what could have been a larger synagogue.[7]

It also appears from the rabbinic literature that Magdala had a synagogue. Next to it was a *beth ha-midrash*, a school for the explanation and application of holy scripture (at all events at the beginning of the second century, perhaps earlier). The city produced two rabbis whose voices can still be heard in the Talmud and the Midrashim. These are Rabbi Isaac of Magdala and Rabbi Judah of Magdala, both from the beginning of the fourth century.

In a midrash on Lamentations 2.2 which begins with the words 'The Lord has destroyed without mercy all the habitations of Jacob', Magdala is cited as an example. The sages give an extensive description of the piety of the town. There were 300 stalls where you could buy the birds necessary for ritual purification. And the religious tax which went to Jerusalem weighed so much that it had to go by wagon. Yet the city was devastated. Why? While the answer to the question given in the case of two other towns is 'disunity' and 'witchcraft', in Magdala 'adultery' is cited as the reason (Ika Rabbah II, 2,4). So the city was not just associated with piety, but also with adultery.

Magdala occurs in the rabbinic literature under different names: as Magdala (citadel), as Migdal Sebayah (tower of dyers) and as Migdal Nunayah (tower of fish). Fréderic Manns has demonstrated that Magdala and Migdal Sebayah are interchangeable, and are identical. Migdal Nunayah occurs just once. Then, too, it is clear that Magdala is being referred to. Migdal Nunayah and Migdal Sebayah probably refer to particular parts of Magdala.[8]

Flavius Josephus, a first-century Jewish historian, scribe and army commander, often speaks of the town of Tarichea. Anyone who takes all his descriptions into account must put Tarichea, too, north of Tiberias, in the same place as present-day Mejdel. In that case Magdala would be the Jewish name of the town and Tarichea its Greek name. At this time a town would often have two names. Greek was the second language, the international language, since Alexander the Great had founded his great empire in the third century before Christ.

Josephus gives the impression that Tarichea was a large town with 40,000 inhabitants. Its fishing fleet consisted of 240 ships. Josephus relates that Tarichea had a hippodrome, a Greek racetrack for horses (*Jewish War* II, 599–608). That was something that not all towns could allow themselves.

Magdala was a prosperous town.

That is also evident from the excavations. The houses in Magdala which have been excavated stand in great contrast to the poor huts which have been uncovered in Capernaum.[9] The various names for Magdala show where the prosperity came from.

A prosperous mercantile town

Magdala means citadel. Josephus mentions the town above all for its strategic situation and its place in the fight against the Romans. Magdala lay directly on the west bank of the Sea of Galilee and was flanked on two sides by rocks. The road along the sea could easily be closed by the inhabitants. Josephus, who was elected governor of Galilee by the rebels at the beginning of the Jewish war, had the town fortified on the landward side (*Jewish War* III, 462–5).

The historian and geographer Strabo of Amaseia, who round about the beginning of our era described the various territories of the Roman empire for the use of future political leaders, mentions Tarichea in his work for another reason. He praises its 'excellent salted fish' (*Geography* XVI, 2,45).

Tarichea was not just chosen arbitrarily as the Greek name for Magdala. Taricheion means a place where fish are dried. The salted, dried, preserved fish would have been an important source of income for Magdala. This fishing industry will also be the background to the Hebrew name Migdal Nunayah (tower of fish) for Magdala.

The fact that Strabo – who was no great traveller and derived his information about notable features above all from Rome and Alexandria – mentions the salted fish of Tarichea indicates its fame, and that the fish was traded even outside Galilee.[10]

Magdala must have had a lively trade. The town was very favourably placed for important trade routes. There was one in the direction of Egypt (the *Via Maris*), one in the direction of Syria, and one in the direction of the Mediterranean Sea. There were also routes to Judaea and to the north.

Strabo also mentions a second characteristic of Tarichea. 'Fruit trees grow there which look like apple trees.'

Josephus tells us rather more. North of Tarichea was a flat area which is called Gennasar (Gennesaret in the New Testament).

Josephus interrupts his account of the bloody and strategic events at the time of the Jewish war to describe the special yield from this plain. He praises the fertility of the soil and the favourable climate, which is particularly suitable for the walnut tree, the palm tree, the olive tree and the fig tree. Moreover the soil produces plants and shrubs which are seldom seen together and bear ripe fruit uninterruptedly. Thus the grapes and the figs are there ten months of the year. This is also possible as a result of the irrigation from a very powerful spring 'which is called Capernaum by the inhabitants' (*Jewish War* III, 516–521).

So we could imagine that among its inhabitants Magdala had farmers who cultivated the fruitful plain of Gennesar, fishermen who were active on the Sea of Galilee, workers in the port and in the fishing industry where the fish was treated and salted, and the merchants who went along with all this.

It has been conjectured that fabric was also dyed in Magdala. That follows from the name Migdal Sebayah: tower of dyers. The dyeing industry of that time used dyes made from plants and fruit. It was also important to have a good deal of water close at hand.[11] Thanks to the Sea of Galilee and the plain of Gennasar, the inhabitants of Magdala had plenty of both.

Magdala had everything it needed to be a prosperous trading town. There could have been trade in salted fish, dyed fabrics and a variety of agricultural products. Moreover the town was very favourably located for different international trade routes and its strategic situation was also strong. However, all this brought the town not only prosperity but also strife.

Hotbed of opposition, sanctuary for fugitives

Mary Magdalene lived at a time when Israel was bowed down

under the Roman occupation. This was an occupation which was also very noticeable in and around Magdala.[12]

From 63 BCE, after a period of relative independence, the land of the Jews began to be incorporated into the Roman empire. That this was not a gentle process is shown by the following passage about determining how much tax was to be paid. The Roman Christian Lactantius writes:

> The Roman tax authorities went all over the place and turned everything upside down. The fields were measured metre by metre, every vine and fruit tree was counted, every head of cattle was registered, and the number of people was noted down precisely. The population was driven into the cities, and all the markets were thronged with families arriving in groups. Everywhere one heard the cries of those who were being interrogated under torture and being beaten. Sons were played off against fathers, women against their husbands. When everything had been checked out, they tortured those liable for tax until they made statements against themselves, and when the pain had won, these people wrote down property liable to tax which did not even exist. Age or state of health were of no importance in all this (*De mortibus Persecutorum* 23.1f.).[13]

Incorporation into the Roman empire met with great opposition from the Jews, and not just because they wanted to be free. There was also a religious background to the opposition. The rebels refused to be governed by foreign rulers who did not practise the religion of Israel. They saw that as a transgression of the law which God himself had established through Moses. Had not Moses said that the king of Israel must not be a foreigner and that he had constantly to study the Law of God (Deut.17.14–20)?

The rebels concluded from this that as a believer one was obliged to refuse to pay the Roman tax with all the consequences that followed. There was a good reason for asking Jesus 'Is it lawful to pay tax to Caesar or not?' (Matt.22.15–22; Luke 20.20–26; Mark 12.13–17).

Josephus wants to persuade his readers that the conviction of the rebels was certainly not generally shared. He writes about one of them, Judas the Galilean,

> In his time a Galilean named Judas tried to stir the natives to

revolt, saying that they would be cowards if they submitted to paying taxes to the Romans, and after serving God alone accepted human masters. This man was a rabbi with a sect of his own, and was quite unlike the others (*Jewish War* II, 118).

However, new revolts kept breaking out, and the terrors did not spare the town of Magdala either.

In 53 BCE a Galilaean revolt against the Romans was put down in Magdala. Josephus relates that on the orders of the Roman Cassius Longinus his soldiers took thirty thousand inhabitants and fugitives prisoner. They were led away and sold as slaves (*Jewish War* I, 180). However, in general it is clear that Josephus is not too precise with his figures. Still ,whether or not it was precisely thirty thousand, Josephus makes it clear that the number was a large one.

From 40 BCE on, Herod the Great – appointed 'King of the Jews' by the Romans – tried to seize power definitively. He became notorious for his cruelty. At the beginning of the conflict a large number of rebels and their families hid in the caves of Arbela close to Magdala. Herod had them smoked out. Many of them were killed n the process. Many also preferred death. They would rather die than be taken prisoner (*Jewish War* I, 310–313).

It is unlikely that Mary Magdalene experienced either event herself. Had she done so, she would certainly have had to be eighty years old when she followed Jesus. However, these stories would surely still have been told in her generation.

Josephus writes about the final rule of Herod the Great:

Herod had the movements of all his subjects investigated, taking away any opportunities they might find for agitation. All their movements were observed. Both in the city and on the roads, there were men who spied on those who met together (*Antiquities* XV, 10,4).

So repression was tangible everywhere, also in Magdala.

Herod's death in 4 BCE brought new revolts. His oldest son Archelaus mourned for seven days in Jerusalem before travelling to Rome to ask the emperor to make a decision on the succession. On the conclusion of the official time of mourning, shortly before the Passover, the feast of liberation from Egypt, there was alternative mourning around the temple among the people assembled there. Now it was not for Herod but for those who shortly beforehand had been burned alive on Herod's orders because they had rejected the placing of a golden eagle in the temple.

Thereupon Archelaus had a whole legion go through the city to break up the crowd offering sacrifices. Three thousand people were killed. He forbade the celebration of the Passover in Jerusalem for that year (*Jewish War* II, 1–13).

Pilgrims from Magdala and the surrounding district will also have been in Jerusalem. They would all have come back home full of this. Perhaps there were also dead and wounded among them to be grieved over.

After the withdrawal of Archelaus, a great rebellion then broke out under the leadership of Judas the Galilean. This revolt, too, only resulted in murder and killing. The Roman Varus came from Syria to help to put it down. With a large army he went through Galilee and headed further south, plundering as he went.

The city of Sepphoris, in a central location close to Nazareth and about twelve miles from Magdala, was razed to the ground. All its inhabitants were carried off and sold as slaves (*Jewish War* II, 66–71).

The emperor Augustus divided the land into three. He appointed one of the sons of Herod the Great over each territory.

In this way Galilee came under the control of Herod Antipas, and with that a period of political stability began.

Unlike his father and his brother, Herod Antipas countered the opposition more with diplomacy than with force. Indeed, he had to, since Rome was sensitive about disturbances in the country. Thus Archelaus was exiled in 6 CE because of his cruelty. Herod Antipas lasted longer, from 4 BCE to 39 CE (*Jewish War* II, 111–12).

Herod Antipas is known especially for the two large cities which he had built in Galilee. Right at the beginning of his government he had the city of Sepphoris rebuilt, and established his seat of government there. Later the city of Tiberias (named after the Roman emperor) rose on the shore of the Sea of Galilee, south of Magdala. These were truly Hellenistic cities, inspired by foreign culture, and offensive in the eyes of the more orthodox Jews. In building Tiberias Herod Antipas certainly took no account whatever of the graves which were located there. As a result of the building of Tiberias Magdala lost its position as the chief town on the sea of Galilee.

Like his brother, Herod Antipas finally had to leave the country and go into exile. His nephew Herod Agrippa, who already ruled over the territories east and north of the Sea of Galilee, was now given rule of the territories of Herod Antipas. In 41 CE Judaea was added to them.

Magdala and Tiberias and the surrounding area both came into the personal possession of Herod Agrippa through the action of the emperor Nero. As a result of that, they both escaped total destruction in the Jewish War.

The Jewish War began in 66. As early as 67 Magdala was captured from the rebels by Vespasian and Titus. Josephus gives a detailed description of the battle. It ends:

> The entire lake was stained with blood and crammed with corpses; for there was not a single survivor. During the days that followed a horrible stench hung over the region. The beaches were thick with wrecks and swollen bodies which, hot and steaming in the sun, made the air so foul that the calamity not only horrified the Jews but revolted even those who had brought it about . . . The dead, including those who earlier perished in the town, totalled 6,700 (*Jewish War* III, 529–31).

Because of the war, at that time Magdala was housing a great many refugees. Vespasian had them separated from the inhabitants on the grounds that they were the ones who had been primarily involved in the war. So that the inhabitants, too, did not take up arms, he allowed the refugees free passage out on condition that they left the town along the road to Tiberias. Once on the road they were forced to enter Tiberias and gather in the stadium. He had the old and those who were physically weak killed immediately. Josephus relates that there were 1,200 of them. He sent 6,000 of the strongest young men to Nero and sold the rest, numbering 30,400, into slavery (*Jewish War* III, 532–42).

If Mary Magdalene was relatively young when she met Jesus, say between twenty and thirty, perhaps at the age of sixty or seventy she herself witnessed the bloody fall of the city where she had been born and brought up or heard about it from others.

It is clear that the crucifixion of Jesus was neither the first nor the last act of violence with which Mary Magdalene was confronted in her life. She grew up in a city in which the Roman occupation was very tangible. Opposition to it and the suffering that it brought will have shaped her from her youth up.

Mary Magdalene's background

Apart from Mary Magdalene, all the Marys in the New Testament can be recognized by their families. Mary the mother of Jesus, Mary the mother of James, Mary of Joses, Mary of James, Mary the sister of Martha and Lazarus, Mary of Clopas . . . and then Mary of Magdala? Our Mary is not named after a father, a relative, a son, a brother or a sister. Perhaps her family was not known to the circle around Jesus. At all events, she was not defined by her family, but by the fact that she came from Magdala.

Should we then think of a Mary of Magdala who sought to please men from near and far? I quoted the only reference to sexual promiscuity in Magdala at the beginning of this section. It is to be found in the Midrash on Lamentations mentioned there. The sages give 'adultery' as the reason for the destruction of Magdala. However, the adultery is mentioned in the context of piety. Despite this piety, Magdala was devastated because of adultery. There is no obvious reason for associating Mary Magdalene in particular with adultery, just as there is no special reason for describing her as extraordinarily pious because of the piety of Magdala.

However, we may allow her name to conjure up the general atmosphere of Magdala. This was the atmosphere of a trading town on an international route, in which people of all kinds of religions and customs met one another at the market. It was the atmosphere of a prosperous town which had to suffer under the Roman occupation and the opposition to it, under the violence and political upheaval which came with the occupation. It was also the atmosphere of a tolerant city, in which both Jewish and Hellenistic culture were known from the inside.

Mary Magdalene owes her name to the Hebrew name for the city. She is specifically called Mary of Magdala and not Mary of Tarichea. This strengthens the impression that she was a Jew.[14]

Mary Magdalene as a disciple of Jesus

The New Testament Gospels agree in telling us that Mary Magdalene was one of the followers of Jesus. She was not the only woman; there were others too. The Gospels do not give us any indication of precisely how this came about. This is what the Gospel of Mark says when the author is relating the crucifixion of Jesus:

> There were also women looking on from afar, among whom were Mary Magdalene, and Mary the mother of James the younger and of Joses, and Salome, who when he was in Galilee, followed him, and ministered to him; and also many other women who came up with him to Jerusalem (Mark 15.40–41; cf. Matt.27.55–56; Luke 8.1–3).

'Following' and 'ministering' are words which go with discipleship.[15] However, it is not clear whether the women belonged to the small group of permanent followers of Jesus or whether they joined these followers for shorter periods. Nor is it clear what role they filled: had they joined Jesus on their pilgrimage to Jerusalem, were they responsible for meeting the material needs of the small group around Jesus, or were they part of it on an equal footing? The evangelists give us very sparse information, and moreover their testimony is not unanimous. Certainly they always mention Mary Magdalene by name first whenever they are talking about the women followers of Jesus.

In this section we shall survey Jesus' attitude to women as indicated by the Gospels in order to be able to say something more about their possible role among his followers. Then we shall investigate Mary Magdalene's function more specifically.

Jesus' view of women

Jesus did not say anything special about the position that women should occupy; at any rate, the New Testament Gospels do not say anything about this. But we can get some idea of Jesus' view of women if we look at the way in which he dealt with things that affected the world of women's experience at that time. He talks about the laws of purity, about marriage and divorce, about motherhood and the family.

The laws of purity related to food, sex, pregnancy and birth; to contact with blood, or with the sick and the dead; really, anything to do with the body. Anyone who had become unclean could make others unclean by physical contact and therefore for the time being was an outcast. The system of purity divided society into categories of clean and unclean. The rules were such that the poor, the sick, foreigners and women in general were regarded as unclean more often and for longer periods than the rich, the healthy, Israelites and males.

Jesus' view stood this division of society on its head. His starting point was that there is nothing that makes a person unclean. Only what comes from the heart can make someone unclean. He says:

> For what comes out of a man is what defiles a man. For from within, out of the heart of a person, come evil thoughts, fornication, theft, murder, adultery, coveting, wickedness, deceit, licentiousness, envy, slander, pride, foolishness. All these evil things come from within, and they defile a person (Mark 7.21–23; cf. Matt.15.18–20).

Jesus spiritualizes physical uncleanness, and this makes the starting point for men and women in principle equal not only in religious but also in social matters, in contrast to what was customary in the time of Jesus.[16]

At that time, after a marriage the initiative for divorce lay above all with the husband. A woman could be sent away for all kinds of reasons, and this made her social position uncertain. Here too Jesus took another line. He refers to the creation story in stating that a husband may not send his wife away. The husband leaves his father and his mother to attach himself to his wife and be one flesh with her. Moses allowed divorce only because of the hardness of people's hearts. Jesus says about this:

Whoever divorces his wife and marries another, commits adultery against her; and if she divorces her husband and marries another, she commits adultery (Mark 10.11–12; cf. Matt.19.9).

In view of this quotation, it is not just the husband who has the initiative. The wife also has a choice. Jesus requires both partners in a marriage to be faithful. The wife is not dependent on whims of her husband. Both bear equal responsibility for their marriage.

A mother who had a son was highly respected at the time of Jesus, certainly the mother of a son who had a religious role. So it could happen that a woman exclaimed to Jesus:

'Blessed is the womb that bore you, and the breasts that you suckled.'
But he said, 'Indeed, blessed are those who hear the word of God and keep it' (Luke 11.27–28).

Jesus' answer is quite remarkable at first sight. With the word 'indeed' he acknowledges that the woman is right.[17] It is the introduction to a confirmation of her words. But what Jesus says seems to be about something quite different. We find the key to understanding Jesus' answer in Isaiah. There it is said about the time when God will show his glory:

And you shall suck, you shall be carried upon her hip, and dandled upon her knees. As one whom his mother comforts, so I will comfort you (Isa.66.12–14).

Jesus makes it clear by whom he thinks he has been suckled and carried. He relates the womb and the breasts about which the woman has spoken to him to God. Life from God determines a person's blessedness. And also the blessedness of a woman.

Elsewhere, too, Jesus extends the blood relationship between indviduals to a relationship on the basis of life with God. When his mother and brothers and sisters have him summoned, he says about the group of people sitting around him:

Here are my mother and my brothers! Whoever does the will of God is my brother, and sister, and mother (Mark 3.34–35; cf. Matt.12.49–50; Luke 8.21).

Jesus breaks through the conventions of his time.[18] He spiritualizes the laws of purity and family ties. He declares marriage to be
a bond between two people who are both responsible and who
both can take initiatives.

Jesus sees men and women as individuals who can be addressed
on equal terms. The important thing is not their physical
cleanness or uncleanness, their family ties and their marriage, but
their disposition: their purity of heart, whether they do God's will
and keep faith with each other. Their physical state does not
determine who they are; on the contrary, what matters is their
spiritual state.

How Jesus treated women

Jesus' view of women can withstand the test of practice, at least
the practice which is related in the Bible. Stories have been
preserved from which we can discover how Jesus related to
women in the last years of his life. These stories confirm what we
have already discovered.

Nowhere do the New Testament Gospels indicate that Jesus
treated women differently from men.

A fine example of this is the story of the Canaanite or Syro–
Phoenician woman whom Jesus meets outside Israel
(Matt.15.21–28; Mark 7.24–30). She asks Jesus to heal her
daughter who is possessed. Jesus refuses to do so because he is
called simply to Israel, that much-tormented people, and not to
outsiders. He says:

> It is not fair to take the children's bread and throw it to the dogs
> (Matt.15.26; Mark 7.27).

To which she replies:

> Yes, Lord, yet even the dogs eat the crumbs that fall from their
> master's table (Matt.15.27; Mark 7.28).

Jesus praises her for what she has said and her daughter is healed
from that moment on.

The same thing happens with the centurion of the Roman army
at Capernaum (Matt.8.5–13; Luke 7.1–10). He asks for Jesus'
help over a sick boy at home. Thereupon Jesus asks him:

Must I come to help him? (Matt.8.7).[19]

Here the reason is not given in so many words, but the suggestion is clear: an outsider has no right to what is due to Israel. Yet here, too, Jesus heals the child because of the centurion's reply:

> Lord, I am not worthy to have you come under my roof; but say the word, and my servant will be healed (Matt.8.8; Luke 7.6b–7).

Jesus takes the foreign woman outside Israel just as seriously as the centurion from the Roman camp near his own home. He is impressed with the faith of both of them. Both children are healed. If any difference in approach were to become evident, it would be here. Jesus listens to the woman, enters into discussion with her and allows himself to be convinced, just as he is by the man.

There are also other stories which indicate that Jesus' conduct was contrary to a variety of norms which were customary for men and women. Thus the scribes and Pharisees bring a woman to Jesus when he is teaching in the temple (John 8.1–11). They tell him that she has been caught in the very act of adultery and thus according to the law of Moses must be stoned. What is striking here is that they do not also bring the man. After all, the pair must have been caught together, and he too should be stoned (Lev.20.10). They do this 'to test him, that they might have some charge to bring against him'. Clearly they know that, confronted with this fact, he could deny the law of Moses. However, Jesus is able to save the woman without getting into the discussion. He says:

> Let him who is without sin among you be the first to throw a stone at her (John 8.7).

Thereupon they depart one by one.

Another example is the story about the woman with an issue of blood (Matt.9.19–22; Mark 5.25–34; Luke 8.43–48). Unclean as she was, she was not expected to touch or be touched by others. However, when she grasps Jesus by his garment in the hope of being healed, he does not let her action go unnoticed. Yet he does the unexpected thing: he praises her faith in public instead of criticizing her action. 'Daughter,' he calls her. She is a daughter of Israel, although according to the prevailing code she has not behaved as such.

There are also stories from which it emerges that Jesus knows the world of women's experience from the inside and takes it seriously. One example of this is the blessing of the children (Matt.19.13–15; Mark 10.13–16; Luke 18.15.17). Children and women belonged together and had no place in public life. When the evangelists relate how many people had eaten the bit of bread and the few fish which Jesus multiplied, they counted only the men. 'Besides women and children', says Matthew to make things clear (Matt.14.21; 15.38). On one occasion when people brought children to Jesus in the hope that he would lay hands on them and pray for them, the disciples sent them away. Jesus had better things to do. But he himself took another view. He put the children at the centre and said:

> Let the children come to me, do not hinder them; for to such belongs the kingdom of God. Truly, I say to you, whoever does not receive the kingdom of God like a child shall not enter it (Mark 10.14–15).

And he indeed laid hands on them.

Another example is the story about Martha and Mary in which Martha feels that she is missing out because there is a lot to do in providing hospitality for Jesus (Luke 10.38–42). She complains to Jesus that her sister Mary is leaving everything to her. It is striking that Martha feels free to tell Jesus what is disturbing her. Evidently she assumes that he will be sympathetic about so to speak domestic questions and will be willing to use his authority. Jesus' answer is disconcerting. It is Mary who has chosen the good thing: she is sitting at his feet and listening to his words. 'Sit at the feet of' is an expression which indicates a teaching situation. Thus we are told that in his youth Paul 'sat at the feet of Gamaliel', from whom he had received his instruction (Acts 22.3).

That Jesus' teaching was meant not only for men but also for women is evident from the fact that in his illustrations and stories he seeks to refer to the experience of both. He speaks just as easily of the pains of giving birth, leaven, salt, light, water and keeping the house clean, as he does of stewardship, keeping sheep, fishing and being a father.

We can see that women were in fact taught by Jesus, not just from the example of Martha and Mary. Jesus' conversation with the Samaritan woman, too, is typically didactic (John 4.1–30). A less well-known but no less striking example can be found at the end of the Gospel of Luke. There the two men in shining garments remind the women at the empty tomb what Jesus had said about his death:

> 'Remember how he told you, while he was still in Galilee, that the Human One must be delivered up into the hands of sinful people, and be crucified, and on the third day rise.' And they remembered his words (Luke 24.7–8).

Anyone who leafs back through the Gospel will see when Jesus said that. Not publicly, but in an intimate moment with the small circle of his disciples. Luke describes it:

> Now it happened that as he was praying alone the disciples were with him; and he asked them, 'Who do the people say that I am?' And they answered, 'John the Baptist; but others say, Elijah; and others, that one of the old prophets has risen.' And he said to them, 'But who do you say that I am?' And Peter answered, 'The Christ of God.' But he charged and commanded them to tell this to no one, saying, 'The Human One must suffer many things, and be rejected by the elders and chief priests and scribes, and be killed, and on the third day be raised' (Luke 9.18–22).

The women who discover the empty tomb thus belong to the small circle of disciples. At least according to Luke.

The women belong among those disciples who were evidently allowed to be with Jesus even when he withdrew into solitude to pray. The women belong among the disciples who hear things and are told things by Jesus which must remain hidden from others.

Women who belong to the small circle of disciples? Then didn't the small circle around Jesus consist of twelve men?

Nowadays it is generally assumed that in the case of the disciples the number twelve has above all a symbolic significance. The twelve stand for the renewal of the people of God, the Jewish people. This is the people of God which at its origin numbered twelve tribes, according to the sons of Jacob, but which in the time of Jesus had only two tribes left. That people found in Jesus someone who created Israel anew: the two tribes again become twelve. We do not know precisely who the twelve disciples were; each evangelist gives a different list of names. Thus the permanent group around Jesus probably consisted of more than twelve disciples. There is general agreement over that. However, scholars are far from being agreed as to whether women, too, belonged to the permanent group of disciples.[20]

Elisabeth Schüssler Fiorenza has coined the phrase 'discipleship of equals'. According to her, no distinction can be made between male and female disciples at the beginning of the Jesus movement. They were all disciples of the one teacher, all brothers and sisters of Jesus. The gospel of the kingdom of God allows no distinction. It was meant for everyone without exception.[21] Jesus' view of women and men as people who must be addressed equally on the basis of their spiritual attitude instead of their physical state argues for a discipleship of equals. The stories about Jesus' dealings with women confirm that image. On the basis of the above considerations we can assume that Jesus made no distinction between men and women. It is unimaginable that Jesus had women with him solely to see to his material needs.

Women as well as men will have been among 'the crowds' which Jesus attracted. They will also have been among the people who went on pilgrimage with Jesus to Jerusalem. However, the New Testament evangelists mention a number of women followers by name. It seems likely that they belonged to the small circle of permanent disciples, with Mary Magdalene first and foremost.

Mary Magdalene as a disciple

To be a disciple of Jesus and to belong to the small group of his permanent followers had far-reaching consequences for everyday life, certainly for a woman. To follow Jesus meant travelling around, leaving everything behind and following him. It meant living in a poverty and simplicity which one had chosen for oneself. It meant having dealings with the other disciples, rich and poor, from the city or the country, whether zealot, toll collector or fisherman. It meant abstaining from sex.[22] It also meant incurring danger from both Jews and Romans. Mary Magdalene had to accept all this in order to follow Jesus. We need to imagine the spirit that characterized Jesus. Then we can understand something of what drove Mary Magdalene.

Jesus went from town to town and village to village to preach the gospel. At the beginning of the Gospel of Mark we read:

> Now after John was arrested, Jesus came into Galilee, preaching the gospel of God, and saying, 'The time is fulfilled, and the kingdom of God is at hand; repent, and believe in the gospel' (Mark 1.14–15).

According to Jesus the moment had arrived when it would actually become evident that God had the power, and not evil. That was the heart of his message. The evangelists relate that he brought this message 'as one who has authority and not like the scribes'. He did not proclaim the kingdom of God simply by referring to the scriptures. His authority emerged from the fact that he matched words with deeds. He showed that God had the power, and did so by driving out evil spirits.

In Jesus' time, there was widespread belief in the existence of evil spirits. They were servants of Satan, just as the angels were servants of God. They tried to seduce people to sin, could dominate and destroy someone's personality, and could cause sicknesses. We could now say that 'evil spirits' were the powers who were opposed to God's purpose for creation.

Jesus drove out evil spirits. Not through magic, as was customary in his time (even among the scribes), but through the power of the word of God. In doing this he did not make himself popular with everyone. His family thought that he was 'out of his mind' and the scribes said that he drove out spirits 'by the prince of the evil spirits' (Mark 3.21).

Jesus says of this:

> No one can enter a strong person's house and plunder his goods, unless he first binds the strong person; then indeed he may plunder his house (Mark 3.27).

The fact that the evil spirits have no power over Jesus makes it clear that he has bound the prince of the evil spirits and that God's rule is effectively breaking through in him. With Jesus, the 'glory of the Lord' has come:

> The blind receive their sight, the lame walk, lepers are cleansed, and the deaf hear, the dead are raised and the poor have good news preached to them . . . (Luke 7.22; cf. Matt.11.5 and Isa.35.5–6).

In this sense, too, Jesus appears with authority. He knows that he is a special messenger from God. That means that where necessary he acts independently of the tradition, above all where the tradition goes against his conviction that God, who is the creator of all, has mercy on all without distinction.[23] So he says:

> You have heard that it was said, 'You shall love your neighbour and hate your enemy.' But I say to you, Love your enemies and pray for those who persecute you, so that you may be daughters and sons of your Father who is in heaven; for he makes his sun rise on the evil and on the good, and sends rain on the just and on the unjust (Matt.5.43–45; cf. Luke 6.35).

On the basis of the kingdom of God which has come near, Jesus calls on men and women to repent and believe. He summons them to have a fundamental trust in God's rule and, in connection with this, a new lifestyle. This new lifestyle is characterized by detachment from everything with which the compulsive self is occupied and by entering into the service of the kingdom of God in a disinterested way (Luke 12.22–31; Matt.11.28–30). Trust in God's rule brings release. There is no longer any reason for anxiety, for hurt, for anger, for a display of power, for clinging to earthly goods, for vengeance, for anxiety, for nursing guilt. There is every reason to live lovingly in freedom.

On the one hand this life-style is a consequence of trust in the breakthrough of the kingdom of God. On the other hand this new life-style also makes that kingdom of God grow. Thus Jesus says:

> With what can we compare the kingdom of God, or what parable shall we use for it? It is like a grain of mustard seed, which, when sown upon the ground, is the smallest of all the seeds on earth; yet when it is sown it grows up and becomes the greatest of all shrubs, and puts forth large branches, so that the birds of the air can make nests in its shade (Mark 4.30–32).

The seed that is sown is trust, from which true life grows. Alternatively, the seed which is sown is Jesus himself, from whom true life grows. Thus the seed brings forth fruit. To live from Jesus in whom the kingdom of God breaks through makes the kingdom grow.

What moved Mary Magdalene to follow Jesus? She will have come under the spell of his authority, like so many others. But we can say yet more in view of what we have so far come to know about her.

She had grown up in a city in which the Roman occupation, the opposition to it and the suffering which that brought were tangible. That could have made her receptive precisely to the non-violent, the spiritual and the healing element of the kingdom of God as this took shape in Jesus.

She had grown up in a place where Jewish and Hellenistic culture lived side by side. She had also grown up with people from different countries and of different religions who came to Magdala with their trade. That could have made her receptive to Jesus' emphasis on people's dispositions, on their inner life and the way in which they really acted, rather than external differences. And this could have made her receptive to the conviction that God has mercy on all without distinction, because God is a God of the whole creation: the God of human beings is also the God of nature, which particularly around Magdala proved to be so abundant and rich.

Ambivalence

Anyone who tries to imagine that the small group around Jesus in fact consisted of men and women inevitably comes up against the question why the evangelists pay so little attention to the fact. Nowhere do they use the feminine form of the Greek word for disciple. Not once do they report that Jesus was attacked for having female followers. Nothing is said about their calling. Clearly a veil of mystery hangs over the women. Read, for example, the Gospel of Mark. Only at the end of the Gospel do we discover, very abruptly, that women, too, had followed Jesus from the beginning of his public ministry. Suddenly the readers become aware that the whole Gospel has given them the wrong idea here. Everything that they have read about the disciples must be revised. Whenever they are discussed, both men and women must be kept in mind. Yet the Gospel mentions the women only when it cannot avoid doing so, just before the cross and resurrection. That is strange.

The same ambivalence can be felt in the Gospels of Matthew and Luke.

As I remarked earlier, the Gospel of Matthew and the Gospel of Luke both used the Gospel of Mark as a source. A comparison shows that these two evangelists differ from Mark where the women followers are concerned. Mark related:

> There were also women looking on from afar, among whom were Mary Magdalene, and Mary the mother of James the younger and of Joses, and Salome, who, when he was in Galilee, followed him, and ministered to him; and also many other women who came up with him to Jerusalem (Mark 15.40–41).

Matthew turns this into:

> There were also many women there, looking on from afar, who had followed Jesus from Galilee, ministering to him; among whom were Mary Magdalene, and Mary the mother of James and Joseph, and the mother of the sons of Zebedee (Matt.27.55–56).

There are important differences. Mark speaks of two groups of women. The individual women mentioned by name followed and served Jesus when he was still in Galilee. The other women went with Jesus on pilgrimage to Jerusalem. By contrast Matthew is talking about one group of women. They follow Jesus from Galilee and not earlier. There is no mention of both following and serving, but of following with the aim of serving. Matthew thus puts the women mentioned by name in the large group of the many anonymous women. And here he leaves open precisely what their role is. The author seems to want to say: they only began to follow Jesus from Galilee and then not with the aim of learning from him but with the aim of serving him. Later, however, Mary Magdalene and the other Mary seem to be familiar with Jesus' teaching. Here 'serve a rabbi' can be used as a synonym for 'learn from a rabbi'.[24]

Luke, who is concerned to relate everything 'in due order' (Luke 1.3), brings the women forward by comparison with Matthew, as was to be expected. They do not appear at the crucifixion, but right at the beginning of the journey which Jesus makes with the Twelve in Galilee. In Luke the Twelve are the twelve apostles whom Jesus has chosen from his many disciples (Luke 6.13). Luke relates:

> Soon afterwards he went on through cities and villages, preaching and bringing the good news of the kingdom of God. And the twelve were with him, and also some women who had been healed of evil spirits and infirmities: Mary, called Magdalene, from whom seven evils spirits had gone out, and Joanna, the wife of Chuza, Herod's steward, and Susanna, and many others, who provided for them out of their means (Luke 8.1–3).

Luke brings the healings to the fore as a new fact. Seven evil spirits are said to have been cast out from Mary Magdalene, and we shall be returning to that shortly. Luke is in part clearer than Matthew, but he too is somewhat ambivalent.

In Luke it is clear what 'serve' means. Luke's use of the word cannot mean 'be taught by a rabbi'. In Luke the women serve not just the rabbi but the whole group.[25]

The ambivalence in Luke arises from the obscurity caused by his sentence construction. Precisely what is the function of the three women mentioned by name? Do they belong with the Twelve, and are they present with Jesus, as the Twelve are, whenever he is preaching the gospel of the kingdom of God? Or do they belong with the many women who serve the group with what they can count as their possessions? The sentence construction allows both interpretations, and the Gospel does not make things any clearer. On the one hand it seems to talk about a homogeneous group of women. The account of the resurrection speaks of a group of anonymous women who had prepared the spices (Luke 23.55). They resemble the 'many women' in Luke 8.3. Later the women who are mentioned by name also seem to belong with them (Luke 24.10). Only Susanna is not among them. That should argue for one large group of women. On the other hand we cannot assume that 'many women' could have remembered Jesus' words about his suffering and resurrection (cf. Luke 24.8; 9.18–22). That would again argue for a distinction between the women mentioned by name and the 'many other women'.

Is it inattentiveness that makes the first three Gospels seem so unclear about the women followers of Jesus? I think that the opposite is the case. The evangelists felt that their story about Jesus would not carry conviction if they put too much emphasis on the fact that Jesus also included women in the small group of his permanent followers.

Not only the Jewish tradition but quite certainly also the Roman Empire emphatically propagated marriage and motherhood as the only proper way in which a woman should spend her life. Since the emperor Augustus, Roman legislation had aimed at allowing as many women as possible to marry. The birth-rate was declining. Children had to be brought into the world.[26]

It was presumably with a view to making a good impression on outsiders that the Gospels preferred to hint at the way in which Jesus had women disciples among his permanent followers rather than to do complete and unambiguous justice to historical reality. It is also quite possible that the first Christians, who were just as much conditioned by their culture as anyone else, could not get on very well with women disciples once they no longer had the earthly leadership of Jesus.

Mary Magdalene as a key witness

It is clear why the New Testament evangelists nevertheless mention the women. They are important witnesses: witnesses to the crucifixion, the burial, the empty tomb and the revelation about it. They are the ones who can bear witness that Jesus had really died, that he had been put in the tomb, that the tomb had been closed and that to their great consternation the tomb later proved open and empty. After the Roman authorities, they were the only ones who could refute the story going the rounds that 'his disciples have stolen the body' (Matt.28.11–15).

Women as witnesses. However, that was not convincing either in the Jewish or the Roman tradition.[27] Moreover Paul omits the women. He mentions witnesses only in connection with the resurrection. And then Cephas (Aramaic for Peter) and the Twelve are the first. Paul then goes on to mention 'brothers' and 'apostles' as witnesses. He may perhaps also mean women by that, but this is improbable. Only the church fathers of the second century again speak about the women. They try to find an answer to the question why the risen Christ appeared to them in particular.

Women as witnesses: it has to be a historical fact, since the very idea is unthinkable in the traditions I have mentioned.[28]

It is also credible. Precisely when one person is taken less seriously than another, there can be more free play. All the disciples had at first fled on Jesus' arrest (Mark 14.50). Peter made an attempt to keep close to Jesus, but he too found the situation too hot (Mark 14.54, 66–72). Then the women come into the picture (Mark 15.40–41). The others keep clear. The women run a very real danger. Jesus was not condemned for just any crime. He was condemned as 'king of the Jews', as posing a danger to the Roman empire. That means that his followers ran the risk of being condemned to death just as he had been. It was not that the women among his followers were not in any danger.[29] However, they could have hoped that they were more inconspicuous than the men.

Women as witnesses. The evangelists mention various names in this connection. They have one name in common, Mary Magdalene, and they always name her first.[30] She is even the only woman to be named in the Gospel of John in connection with the resurrection. So we can call Mary Magdalene the key witness.

A woman as key witness. In this section we shall look at the different ways in which each Gospel deals with that fact.

The Gospel of Mark: anxiety

The Gospel of Mark relates that Mary of Magdala, Mary of James and Salome went to Jesus' tomb to anoint his body. The three women anxiously ask themselves who will be able to roll away the stone from the tomb. However, when they look up, they see from afar that the stone has already been rolled away. They enter the tomb and are quite startled when they see someone sitting in the tomb in a white garment. He says to them:

> You seek Jesus of Nazareth, who was crucified. He has risen, he is not here; see the place where they laid him. But go, tell his disciples and Peter. 'He is going before you into Galilee.' There you will see him, as he told you (Mark 16.6–7).[31]

This is a reminder of a promise made earlier by Jesus (Mark 14.28). The reaction of the women is quite remarkable.

> And they went out and fled from the tomb; for trembling and astonishment had come upon them; and they said nothing to any one, for they were afraid (Mark 16.8).

These sentences form the conclusion to the Gospel of Mark as we know it. However, there is a debate as to whether the Gospel originally ended with the women fleeing and keeping silent. Perhaps the real conclusion to the Gospel has been lost.[32]

A number of scholars think that in terms of narrative technique the Gospel could have ended very meaningfully with v.8.[33] The Gospel puts Peter and Mary Magdalene side by side (Mark 16.1–8; 14.66–72).[34] Both fail. In both their cases, anxiety gains the upper hand. Both are examples of the fulfilment of the prophecy of Zechariah of which Jesus reminds them shortly before his arrest. He says:

> You will all fall away; for it is written, 'I will strike the shepherd, and the sheep will be scattered' (Mark 14.27; cf. Zech 13.7).

However, for the readers, both are also examples of people who have overcome their failure and their anxiety. Mary Magdalene and the women eventually did speak and Peter and the others recovered from their denial. Otherwise the readers would not have known about the resurrection. However, the Gospel of Mark does not end with the overcoming of anxiety but with anxiety. Its conclusion relates to the difficult situation of persecution faced by the first Christians. Anxiety was everywhere. The conclusion of the Gospel has a literary focus. The anxiety is understandable: not only anxiety about other human beings, but also anxiety at the miracle of the resurrection. But the proclamation of the gospel depends on overcoming the anxiety. The abrupt end of the Gospel of Mark makes a powerful impact on readers: they are not to keep silent, but to speak. And indeed they are to go to Galilee, where Jesus unfolded his teaching. He is going before them on this way; they will see him there.

The Gospel of Matthew: faith

The Gospel of Matthew has two, not three, women going to the tomb: Mary Magdalene and the other Mary. Perhaps the other Mary is the same as Mary of Joseph from the Gospel of Mark. It is also possible that she is the mother of Jesus.

The Gospel of Matthew does not take over the emphasis on anxiety in Mark. In Matthew faith occupies the central place. The Gospel relates that Mary of Magdala and the other Mary are at the burial of Jesus, 'sitting opposite the sepulchre' (Matt.27.61). The next time we hear of them they are going to look at the tomb (Matt.28.1). They do not go to anoint the body of Jesus but to look at the tomb. Thus the reader gets the impression that the two Marys have remained at the tomb all this time, in the expectation that something special is going to happen to it.[35] This impression is reinforced by the fact that in the intervening verses the evangelist introduces the high priests and Pharisees, who remind themselves that Jesus has said that he will be raised after three days (Matt.27.62–66). Thereupon the tomb is secured by Pilate and guards come to stand by it. However, as soon as the two Marys go to visit the tomb, the earth shakes. An angel rolls the stone away from the tomb and sits on it as if it were a throne. The guards are so overcome by fear that they fall down as though dead. The two Marys are also afraid, but their joy overcomes their fear. They immediately depart from the tomb to do what the angel required of them:

> Go quickly and tell his disciples, 'He has risen from the dead, and behold, he is going before you to Galilee; there you will see him' (Matt.28.7b).[36]

The two Marys see Jesus before that. He comes to meet them. They take hold of his feet and worship him. He too asks them to go to 'my brothers'. They will see him in Galilee. Then the eleven go to Galilee. There they worship Jesus, but some doubt. Coming closer Jesus says to them:

> Go therefore and make disciples of all nations, baptizing them in the name of the Father and of the Son and of the holy spirit, teaching them to observe all that I have commanded you; and lo, I am with you always, to the close of the age (Matt.28.19–20).

The mission charge given to the two Marys was addressed to the eleven. The eleven receive the charge to go to 'all nations'.

The Gospel of Luke: *seven evil spirits*

The Gospel of Luke follows Mark in giving the reason for the visit to the tomb. The women go to the tomb to anoint the body of Jesus. In Mark and Matthew we had to think of two or three women; in Luke we do not know the precise number. For him these are the women 'who had come with Jesus from Galilee' (Luke 23.55). Possibly they are the 'many women' from Luke 8.1–3. Luke tones down the anxiety in Mark so that it becomes 'perplexity'. The women are perplexed when they find the tomb empty. Two men in shining garments remind them that Jesus himself had said that he had to suffer and rise. He had already said this in Galilee (9.18–22). It is remarkable that in Luke, in contrast to Mark and Matthew, the women are not told to say anything to the others. They go to the apostles of their own accord to tell them everything. However, they are not believed. Nor do they need to be believed, since what they have to relate does not add anything. Jesus appears to Peter, the two disciples on the Emmaus road and then to the eleven and those who were with them. He opens their minds so that they can understand the scriptures. He says:

> Thus it is written, that the Christ should suffer and on the third day rise from the dead, and that repentance and forgiveness of sins should be preached in his name to all nations, beginning from Jerusalem. You are witnesses to these things. And behold, I send the promise of my Father upon you; but stay in the city, until you are clothed with power from on high (Luke 24.46–49).

Where in Matthew the mission charge 'to all nations' is addressed to the eleven, in Luke it is addressed to the eleven 'and those who were with them' (Luke 24.33). On the basis of Luke 8.1–3 we may assume that Mary Magdalene and the other women were also 'with them'. But on the basis of Acts 1.14 we must assume that Luke wants to make us believe that Jesus was concerned only with the apostles 'whom he had chosen'.

The most striking feature in Luke is a fact that he adds about Mary Magdalene which is new by comparison with Mark and Matthew. The women mentioned by name in Luke 8.1–3 are said to have been healed from evil spirits and from sicknesses. Luke does not describe the ailments of any of the three women apart from Mary Magdalene: seven evil spirits are said to have gone out of her. So Luke indicates very precisely what has happened to Mary Magdalene: not one (Luke 4.35) nor a legion of demons (Luke 8.30) has gone out of her, but seven.

The number can indicate totality. In that case Mary Magdalene would have been totally possessed and have been completely healed by Jesus.[37] Perhaps we must then imagine her as being like the man who was possessed by a legion of demons. It is said of him:

> For a long time he had worn no clothes, and he lived not in a house but among the tombs . . . he was kept under guard, and bound with chains and fetters, but he broke the bonds and was driven by the demon into the desert (Luke 8.27–29).

However, it is also possible that the evil spirits refer to physical sickness. In addition to the seven evil spirits of Mary Magdalene Luke also has Jesus giving teaching in which he speaks of seven evil spirits. If we apply that to Mary Magdalene, we could suppose that she was to blame for the seven demons, because she had not armed herself sufficiently after a first liberation. Jesus says:

> When a strong man fully armed guards his own palace, his goods are in peace; but when one stronger than he assails him and overcomes him, he takes away his armour in which he trusted, and divides his spoil. He who is not with me is against me, and he who does not gather with me scatters. When the unclean spirit has gone out of a person, he passes through waterless places seeking rest; and finding none he says, 'I will return to my house from which I came.' And when he comes he finds it swept and put in order. Then he goes and brings seven other spirits more evil than himself, and they enter and dwell there; and the last state of that person becomes worse than the first (Luke 11.21–26).

Quite another possibility is that Luke, who has 'followed all things closely for some time past' and is more in touch with the Greek world than Matthew, has drawn on a Hellenistic-Christian source for Mary Magdalene's seven evil spirits (Luke 1.3). According to Hellenistic thought the soul consists of eight parts. These are the capacity to feel, to hear, to touch, to taste and to see, the capacity to desire and the capacity to speak. The eighth part is the 'commander'; it has the task of keeping these different capacities in check and giving direction. However, each part tries to gain power for itself. The aim of human life is to get free of these claims to power and thus to achieve a life in harmony with the divine.[38] The fact that precisely seven evil spirits are said to have gone out of Mary would then show that she had gone far along this way.

Be this as it may, Luke can make good use of the seven evil spirits and the other healings. He can also explain the fact that not only the twelve male apostles permanently followed Jesus but also the three women. The men did that as a result of their calling, as was already clear (Luke 6.12–16). Luke is now suggesting that the women do so out of gratitude. Jesus had healed them. But perhaps he means more. Luke could have drawn from the same source for the healings of Joanna and Susanna as he did from the seven evil spirits. If this source indeed represents Hellenistic thought, we could suppose that the text meant that Jesus had made the women specially capable of following him. The Hellenistic Jewish thinker Philo of Alexandria (beginning of the first century) writes:

> The soul has, as it were, a dwelling, partly men's quarters, partly women's quarters. Now for the men there is a place where properly dwell the masculine thoughts (that are) wise, sound, just, prudent, pious, filled with freedom and boldness, and kin to wisdom. And the women's quarters are a place where womanly opinions go about and dwell, being followers of the female sex. And the female sex is irrational and akin to bestial passions, fear, sorrow, pleasure and desire, from which ensue incurable weaknesses and indescribable sicknesses *(Questions and Answers on Genesis* IV.15).[39]

The terms 'male' and 'female' are used in a metaphorical sense. At the same time they also relate to real men and women. The man is the symbol for reason and the woman for perception through the senses. Men are 'manly' by disposition and women are 'womanly'. However, women can be made 'manly' and men can degenerate into womanliness'.[40] Just as it is the intention that men should rule over women, so it is also the intention that the manly should dominate the womanly. The understanding must regulate sensual perception, among both men and women. If that does not happen, then illnesses (psychosomatic illnesses?) develop. Those who are able to control womanly knowledge are to be called blessed. However, that is reserved only for 'spirits full of the Law'.[41] Perhaps this notion originally underlies the women healed by Luke. Jesus (indeed a 'spirit full of the Law') healed the sicknesses which were part of their femininity. He banished the evil spirits which were part of their womanly weakness. By following him they could now become 'manly', just like the male disciples.[42]

It is improbable that Luke interpreted the seven evil spirits and the other healings of women in such a way, since in Acts he clearly makes the male apostles take the lead and we hear no more about women possibly being made 'men'.[43]

The Gospel of John: persistence

As I remarked earlier, the Gospel of John goes completely its own way. In this Gospel, too, just as in Mark and Matthew, we meet Mary Magdalene first at the crucifixion of Jesus. But in contrast to these, and in a different way from Luke, she does not stand gazing from afar off; we find her close to the cross, within speaking distance (John 19.26–27). John describes it like this:

> But standing by the cross of Jesus were his mother, and his mother's sister, Mary of Clopas, and Mary the Magdalene (John 19.25).

Here John could mean either three or four women. In that case Mary of Clopas is the name of his mother's sister. In both cases we know that John reckons Mary Magdalene among the closest acquaintances of Jesus. In contrast to the three other evangelists, John says nothing about following or serving, nothing about discipleship.

However, the summary given by this text can also be read as a parallelism:

> His mother and his mother's sister
> – Mary of Clopas and Mary the Magdalene.

In that case Mary of Clopas is the name of Jesus' mother and Mary Magdalene is her sister. This interpretation seems unacceptable at first sight, since the two sisters then have the same first name. However, the Greek word translated 'sister' can also mean 'sister-in-law' or 'niece'.[44] Anyone who reads two women out of v.25, will then discover more about Mary Magdalene in v.26. This verse runs:

> When Jesus saw his mother, and the disciple whom he loved standing near, he said to his mother, 'Woman, behold your son.' Then he said to the disciple, 'Behold, your mother.' And from that hour the disciple took her to his own home (John 19.26–27).

In the exegesis which presupposes two women under the cross, Mary Magdalene is the same person as 'the disciple whom Jesus loved'. For the reader who sees verses 25 and 26 following closely one after the other, this is the most logical way of reading them: apart from Jesus there are only two other people present by the cross, and no more. Mary Magdalene is the one who is to be a son to the mother of Jesus (cf. Ruth 4.15).[45] The account of the resurrection suggests the same thing to the reader. Mary Magdalene goes to the tomb, sees that the stone sealing it has been taken away and then goes to get Simon Peter and with him 'the disciple whom Jesus loved'. Those who may already have suspected that Mary Magdalene could be 'the disciple whom Jesus loved' in John 19.25 now have their suspicions confirmed after this further mention of 'the other disciple whom Jesus loved'. This figure would be the mysterious unknown figure who often appears in the Gospel (e.g. John 13.23–25; 21.21–24). However, anyone who maintains this reading must also accept that John is very mysterious about the beloved disciple in 19.26, since 'the disciple who' has a masculine connotation in Greek, as in 20.2. That seems to be going too far. So we shall not be pursuing the matter further.

John is not clear about what happens beneath the cross. The evangelist does not indicate how many women were there. So in our conclusion we shall go no further than to say that in John 19.25–26 Mary Magdalene is depicted as one of the closest acquaintances of Jesus. We shall leave out of account precisely which women are mentioned in 19.25 and who the beloved disciple could be.

However, on the basis of the resurrection narrative we do come to the conclusion that Mary Magdalene is one of the beloved disciples of Jesus.

That Jesus' love was not limited to one or two emerges from the earlier indication in John that he also loved Martha, her sister and Lazarus (John 11.5). Jesus loved 'his own' (John 13.1 and 15.9–17). And 'his own' are the sheep who listen to his voice, who recognize his voice as that of the good shepherd and are guided by him to seek good pastures (John 10.1–10). That Mary Magdalene is one of 'his own' emerges from the fact that she recognizes Jesus' voice and listens to his words (John 20.16–18). Moreover she calls him 'Rabbouni', which means 'my teacher'.[46]

What is most typical about John's description of Mary Magdalene is the emphasis placed by the Gospel on her persistence. This happens in two ways: first of all, she remains at the tomb although the others have gone away; and secondly, she wants to cling to Jesus as she has known him, in his earthly form. In the course of the resurrection narrative she also went to the tomb for this reason. Not to anoint the body as in Mark and Luke; not to see whether Jesus had indeed risen, as in Matthew; but to seek comfort in his physical proximity (John 20.11,13).

John does not depict her so much as the key witness to the empty tomb: Peter and the other disciples get there very quickly. The Gospel presents her as the key witness to the precise meaning of Jesus' resurrection. Thanks to her persistence, she is the one who teaches that it is not a matter of 'holding'. Jesus says:

> Do not hold me, for I have not yet ascended to the Father; but go to my brethren and say to them, I am ascending to my Father and your Father, to my God and your God (John 20.17).[47]

Jesus' resurrection does not mean that he is there after his death as the disciples have known him. He will be with the Father, invisible to the world, only to be experienced by those who love him and keep his commandments. Mary Magdalene has to stand on her own feet. After all, Jesus had said:

> You know the way where I am going . . . I am the way, and the truth, and the life; no one comes to the Father but by me (John 14.4–7).

Jesus asks her to stop holding the visible teacher, but to keep holding on to his teaching, his commandments. His Father will also prove to be her Father, and his God will also prove to be her God. She must go and tell this to her brothers and sisters: Jesus' Father, your Father; Jesus' God, your God (cf. Ruth 1.16).

The Gospel of John is the only Gospel that goes on to make Mary Magdalene say, 'I have seen the Lord!' This is the formulation which Paul uses to legitimate his apostolate.

We cannot infer from this Gospel how Mary's message was received by the brothers and sisters, There are no words which had already been spoken to her earlier, as was the case with Mark, Matthew and Luke.[48] It is certainly clear how the author regards the message of Mary Magdalene. At the beginning of the Gospel, in the introduction, we read about the purpose of Jesus; he has come so that all those who accept Jesus receive from him the possibility of becoming children of God (John 1.12–13). Mary Magdalene may proclaim the crucial message of the gospel with the words 'my brothers and sisters' and 'my Father, your Father'.

Mary Magdalene

Now that we have surveyed the earliest sources for our quest for Mary Magdalene, at the end of this chapter we return to the questions with which we started. Who was Mary Magdalene and what is her story?

Who was she?

Mary Magdalene came from the town of Magdala, by the sea of Galilee; it was a centre of trade on an international route, where people of all kinds of religions and customs met one another at the market. It was a prosperous town where trade was done in salt fish, dyed material and a selection of agricultural products. It was a tolerant town, where both Jewish and Hellenistic culture were known from the inside. It was a fortified town in a strategic location, in an area which suffered much under the Roman occupation and opposition to it. By contrast, nature was rich and abundant in the region. Mary Magdalene's background was in all probability Jewish. However, she is not defined by her family ties as is the case with the other Marys in the four Gospels. She is defined by the city of Magdala from where she comes. From her youth upward she was familiar with violence, with poverty and riches, with injustice, with different cultures and religions, all this in a splendid and extraordinarily fertile natural environment. At a particular moment she began to follow Jesus. It is not inconceivable that she met him in the synagogue at Magdala. Luke is the only Gospel which relates that through Jesus seven evil spirits went out of her. We do not know precisely what that says about her, except that contact with Jesus must have been very liberating and uplifting for her. John depicts her as one of the closest acquaintances of Jesus. She stood just beneath the cross with his family. On the basis of Mark's description of the women at the cross, on the basis of what the Gospels show us about Jesus' attitude towards women, and on the basis of the resurrection stories in Luke and John, we conclude that Mary Magdalene must have belonged to the small circle of disciples who were Jesus' permanent followers. She was under the impact of his authority and his message about the coming of the kingdom of God. She was under the impact of his teaching: the importance that he attached to a good disposition in people rather than to good external behaviour, and also the emphasis that he placed on the overflowing goodness of God, not limited to some but addressed to all.

The evangelists mention Mary Magdalene in their story about Jesus because she is the key witness to his death, to the burial of his body, the empty tomb and the revelation which goes with it. We have seen that her presence at Jesus' tomb showed courage in the face of both the Jewish and the Roman authorities.

It is striking that Mark, Luke and John invite the reader to compare Mary Magdalene with Peter.[49] In Mark she is on the same footing as Peter; in Luke Peter is clearly more important than Mary Magdalene, whereas in John, Peter pales by comparison.[50]

What is her story?

John is the only evangelist who makes Mary Magdalene speak. She says, 'I have seen the Lord'. Matthew and Luke do not reproduce any of her sayings, but relate that she reported what she noticed at the empty tomb. In Matthew and Luke this is a repetition of what the disciples had already been told earlier by Jesus himself. In John it is something new, the crucial significance of Jesus' time on earth: the reader of the Gospel knows of this, but the disciples as a group have still to experience it. In Mark, Mary Magdalene is silent.

As for the content, in Mark and Matthew this is a command: the disciples must go to Galilee. This is the fulfilment of a promise which Jesus gave the disciples before his death. Perhaps we may interpret this figuratively as well as literally. The disciples must hold on to what Jesus had taught them in Galilee. Then they will see him. In Luke it is a memory. The women remember that Jesus prophesied his suffering, death and resurrection as something that had to happen. In John it is a summons to be supported by the spiritual presence of Jesus and to stand on one's own feet as sons and daughters of God.

The evangelists go very different ways in interpreting the function of Mary Magdalene's message. In Matthew her message is meant for the eleven male disciples who along with Judas symbolize the twelve tribes of Israel. Her message has an effect. The eleven indeed go to Galilee. Luke makes it clear that Mary Magdalene delivers her message on her own initiative 'to the eleven and all the others'. Her message gives them the wrong impression. What the women tell is seen as 'foolish talk' (24.11). In John her message is of crucial importance and meant not just for the eleven disciples but for all those who accept Jesus as the light of the world (John 1.18).

To sum up: Matthew portrays Mary Magdalene as a disciple and an apostle before the apostles. Luke makes it clear that while she and the other women are disciples, they have not been called to apostleship like the twelve male disciples. John depicts Mary Magdalene specifically as a disciple and apostle. Mark calls on his readers to become not just disciples but apostles, both men and women, after the fashion of Peter and Mary Magdalene.

In Mark, Matthew and Luke, at the resurrection there are sayings which the disciples as a group had already known before Jesus' death. In the case of John there is a new testimony which Mary Magdalene alone hears, and which is given by the Risen Christ.

It is also striking that John attaches much more importance to Mary Magdalene than Luke does, and at the same time changes the position of Peter.

In the next chapter we shall be looking at texts about Mary Magdalene down to the fourth century, when the emperor Constantine was converted to Christianity and the church became an instrument of power as well as an institution of faith.

3

The Search Continued

From a world I am released through a world,
and from a model through a model which is from the side of
*   heaven.*
And the fetter of oblivion is temporal.
(Gospel of Mary 16.21–17.4)

In the previous chapter we looked at the earliest texts in which Mary Magdalene appears. These are texts which were handed down carefully over the centuries, since they were experienced as God-given and inspired. In this chapter we shall also meet texts which have been carefully preserved: the texts of the church fathers. But we shall also be confronted with texts which have not been preserved, texts which got lost in the course of time, and which were quite firmly stamped 'not part of the church tradition'.

This confronts us with the question why the church tradition thought it worthwhile to preserve some texts and not others.

At the beginning of this chapter it is important for us to realize that early Christianity was very diverse. The followers of Jesus went all over the Roman empire. The Christian faith came into contact with expressions of different cultures: Egyptian, Iranian-Babylonian, Greek, Syrian, African, and so on. In this way different forms of belief came into being and, in connection with them, different writings. These writings were important to the groups for which each was intended. However, some writings were circulated more widely, like the four Gospels which have found a place in the New Testament. In this way a mainstream developed. This was not dictated from above. In the first instance, there were no synods at which particular writings were forbidden or commended. Certainly lists were in circulation which described the state of things. However, these lists differed from one another. The first list containing the twenty-seven books which came to form the New Testament dates from the year 367. It was made by Athanasius, Archbishop of Alexandria.

It is only after the event that we can discover motives which presumably played a role in the acceptance of writings into the church tradition. A first motive was the universal recognition of a work. A second was apostolicity: could a work rightly and reasonably appeal to the first witnesses to Christ? A third motive was whether its content was orthodox.[1]

In this chapter we shall look first at these writings which began to represent the church tradition, and then give a say to those writings which had been lost but have come to light again over the last two centuries.

Church tradition

Anyone who goes in search of Mary Magdalene after the New Testament Gospels will at first be disappointed. She does not appear in the other writings of the New Testament, nor in those of the apostolic fathers or the apologists. At least not as Mary Magdalene. Perhaps she appears as Mary. In his letter to the Romans Paul mentions some women missionaries by name, including a Mary. He says of her:

Greet Mary, who has worked hard among you (Rom.16.6).

It is a great pity that so little is known about the popularity of names in particular areas. Thanks to the evidence of the Bible and Josephus we know that the name Mary occurred a good deal in Israel. Nowadays, one reason given for this is the popularity of the Hasmonaean princess Mariamne, the wife of Herod the Great.[2] So this could be a local phenomenon: the name of Mary was popular in Israel but not outside it. Were that the case, it would seem natural to assume that the Mary mentioned by Paul came from Israel, but nothing can be said for certain. According to Paul, Mary 'worked hard' for the community in Rome. This is the same expression that Paul often uses for his own missionary work.[3] If any of the Marys in the New Testament Gospels seems a likely candidate for this missionary work outside Palestine, it must be Mary Magdalene. More than any other Mary, because she had spent her youth in the town of Magdala, she was familiar from the inside with Hellenistic culture and the different nationalities of the Roman empire. The question remains why Paul omits 'Magdalene'. One answer could be that he does not give any further epithet to any of the names that he mentions. Moreover, he does not mention any other Marys.

Mary Magdalene appears again in the second century, sometimes just as Mary; however, in that case it is in a context in which it is clear that she is Mary Magdalene. First of all mention must be made here of the Gospel fragment added later to Mark (Mark 16.9–20). It is said to come from the beginning of the second century. That same century Mary Magdalene appears in the writings of Irenaeus of Lyons. In the third century she is mentioned by Tertullian of Carthage, Hippolytus of Rome, Origen of Alexandria, Pseudo-Cyprian of Carthage, Dionysius of Alexandria and Pseudo-Clement of Rome. In the fourth century there are numerous references to her. The writings of Ambrose of Milan, Jerome of Rome and Augustine of Hippo are representative.

We are not told about what Mary Magdalene had to say, but we do get an impression of how she was regarded.

Disciple and apostle: helper

Tertullian and Hippolytus have no difficulty in firmly calling Mary Magdalene 'disciple' and 'apostle'. That may be said to be a step forward by comparison with the New Testament Gospels. The Gospels certainly portray her as such (with Luke as the exception as far as apostleship is concerned), but nowhere call her apostle or disciple. Tertullian and Hippolytus do. However, there is a catch.

For Tertullian the women who followed Jesus are disciples and helpers.[4] In his work *On Marrying Only Once* it becomes clear what he means by that. Here he is defending the view that remarriage is not allowed. Among other things he shows that the apostles, too, had no spouses. They took women with them who performed services for them, just like the women who accompanied Jesus.[5] Pseudo-Cyprian shares this view. The women in Luke 8.1–3 were taken along by the apostles. They followed them 'to

learn reverence' and to be initiated 'into the service of philan-
thropy'.[6]

Hippolytus in fact calls Mary Magdalene apostle, but does not
do so in a context relating to authority. He says of the women in
Matt.28.1–10:

> Those who were apostles before the apostles, sent by Christ,
> bear good testimony to us . . . Christ himself came to meet
> these women so that they should become apostles of Christ and
> through obedience accomplish what the old Eve failed to
> accomplish. From now on, in humble obedience, they were to
> make themselves known as perfected. O new consolation, Eve
> is called an apostle! (*On the Song of Songs* XXV, 7–6).

The apostolate of the women is limited to the apostles and is
characterized by obedience. Through obedience they can accomplish what Eve failed to accomplish through disobedience. Christ
gave them the possibility of offering the apostles incorruptible
food in place of the apple (cf. Gen.3). Like Tertullian, Hippolytus, too, comes up with the model of the helper. Eve is a good
helper for Adam, who is the leader.[7] Moreover in Hippolytus,
Eve and Adam are symbols of the synagogue and the church. In
his view the synagogue falls silent, whereas the church boasts.[8]

Pseudo-Clement of Rome also does not know female apostles
in the general sense of the word. He assures his readers that when
it came to the universal preaching of the gospel Jesus sent out only
men, and no women with them.[9]

Full of faith

Thus Mary Magdalene was seen especially as a helper. The fact
that she was recognized as a disciple and apostle did not give her
the authority that was attributed to the male disciples and
apostles. That does not mean that she was not respected for her
faith. Both Tertullian and Hippolytus as well as Pseudo-Clement
praise her for her piety. It is striking that all three do so against the
background of Mary's encounter with the risen Lord in John
20.17. In his letter against female and male ascetics living
together, Pseudo-Clement bears witness that even Mary, 'that
very pious woman', was not allowed to touch Jesus' feet. How

then could male ascetics allow themselves to be looked after by women?[10]

Hippolytus praises Mary because she clung to Jesus' feet, with the intention of going with him to heaven. She is a symbol for the synagogue which wants to join the church.[11]

Tertullian calls Mary Magdalene

> that very pious woman who tried to touch him out of love and not out of curiosity or unbelief, like Thomas (*Against Praxeas* 25.2).

This is an interpretation which is quite remarkable compared with that of the later church fathers.

A teacher?

Hippolytus also mentions Mary Magdalene in a quite different connection. In his book *A Refutation of All Heresies* he describes, among other groups, the sect of the Naassenes. He says that the Naassenes claim to have got their teaching through James, the brother of the Lord. James is said to have handed on the teaching to Mary, and she had disseminated it further.[12] This corresponds with what Origen heard. He quotes the Platonist philosopher Celsus who wrote against Christianity. Among other things, Celsus accuses the Christians of arguing with one another. Here he says in particular that he knows of people who follow Mariamne. He knows followers of Martha, of Mariamne and of Salome. It is quite possible that by Mariamne he means Mary Magdalene.[13] That means that Mary Magdalene had followers, not only according to the Naassenes but also according to Celsus. She had disciples. So she was a teacher. Origen replies that he has made a thorough search of these tendencies, within both Christianity and philosophy, but has not been able to find them.[14]

Origen portrays the Mary whom Paul mentions in the Letter to the Romans as a teacher. In commenting on this letter he says:

> 'Greet Mary, who has worked hard in the Lord.' At this point he (Paul) teaches that both women and men must work for the communities of God. For they work when they instruct young

women to be sober, to love their spouses, to bring up children, to be reserved, chaste, to look after their homes, to be good and subordinate to their husbands, to practise hospitality, to wash the feet of the saints and in all chastity to practise all the other things that are written about the duties of women (*Commentary on the Letter to the Romans* X.20).

Origen certainly sees the Mary of the Letter to the Romans as a teacher, but as a teacher of the kind that all women should be: a teacher of young girls. Not in the things of the Lord, but in the duties of women.

Jesus and Mary Magdalene: distance

Nevertheless Mary Magdalene preached the resurrection. The fragment of Gospel attributed to Mark mentions Mary Magdalene, 'from whom he had driven out seven evil spirits', as the first to whom the Risen Christ appears.[15] Irenaeus and Pseudo-Cyprian also mention Mary Magdalene without any hesitation as the first witness to the resurrection.[16] Nor does Hippolytus show any sign of restraint in talking of the women who encountered the Risen Lord. It is Origen for whom Mary Magdalene becomes a problem as a witness to the resurrection. In his *Commentary on John* he wrestles with the question why Mary may not touch Jesus but Thomas may.[17] According to him, Jesus forbade Mary because he had not yet appeared to her as fully risen. In his work against Celsus, Origen counters Celsus' claim that only a hysterical woman saw the risen Jesus and some of his disciples who were deceived by the same witchcraft.[18] He refers to the appearances to the disciples on the Emmaus road and to Thomas to demonstrate that Jesus' appearance cannot have been witchcraft of a dream, since he was physically present. He defends Mary Magdalene by pointing out that there is nothing to suggest that she was hysterical. Moreover Jesus appeared not only to her but to another woman, 'the other Mary'.

Origen feels that he is on weak ground with Mary Magdalene: because she is a woman (the sex is always closely associated with hysteria) and because she may not touch Jesus. Later church fathers felt the same problems. From the fourth century there are plenty of commentaries on John 20.17 which go into these difficulties.[19] The earliest is that of Ambrose. He says:

> And rightly is a woman appointed as messenger to men, so that she, who first brought men the message of sin, should also have been the first to bring the message of the grace of the Lord (*On the Holy Spirit* 3, 11,74).

Mary Magdalene might not touch Jesus because she did not immediately recognize his heavenly state.[20] Jerome mentions that Christ first appeared to a woman to show his humility.[21] Mary Magdalene might not touch his feet because she did not believe in his divinity.[22] Augustine was of the same opinion, though he already has to confess that the question why Mary may not touch Jesus but Thomas may is insoluble. However, he insists that as long as Mary Magdalene did not see Christ on the same level as that of the Father, she might not touch him.[23] Also according to Augustine, Christ first appeared to a woman because the woman was also the first to have brought sin.[24]

The main characteristic of this kind of view is that it emphasizes the distance between Mary Magdalene and Jesus. She stands as a female symbol for Eve. He is divine. Her faith is insufficient and therefore she may not touch him. He emphasizes his humility. The intensity of the moment in the garden as John describes it thus disappears into the background. The same thing happens with her testimony, 'I have seen the Lord'. She is not a witness to the risen Lord in all his glory, since she does not recognize his divinity.

What the desert sands yielded up

Until two centuries ago, we would have found no more than the above about Mary Magdalene in the tradition of the early church. However, from the eighteenth century the desert sand has yielded up papyrus codices in which Mary Magdalene also appears. In 1773 the Codex Askewianus was found, containing the writing Pistis Sophia. In 1896 the Papyrus Berolinensis, containing the Gospel of Mary, came to light, and in 1945 the Nag Hammadi Codices were found with the Gospel of Thomas, the Dialogue of the Saviour, the Gospel of Philip, the Wisdom of Jesus Christ and the First and Second Apocalypses of James. Between those two dates the Gospel of Peter (1886), the Letter of the Apostles (1895) and the Manichaean Psalter (1930) were discovered. So too were two church orders, the Apostolic Church Order (first edition 1843) and the Catholic Teaching of the Holy Apostles (first edition 1854).[25] Many versions of the Acts of Philip have also been found.

Of these writings, the Gospel of Thomas, the Gospel of Mary, the Gospel of Peter, the Letter of the Apostles and the Dialogue of the Saviour are the oldest. They come from the period before 150. The other writings come from the second half of the second and from the third century; the Acts of Philip from the fourth century. A new feature is that Mary Magdalene is introduced speaking. Nevertheless we do not really discover what she had to say, but the questions that she had. The Gospel of Mary is an exception to this. In it Mary Magdalene speaks for pages in order to tell her story. I shall be devoting a separate chapter to this Gospel. In this section we shall be concerned with the picture of Mary Magdalene given by the other recently discovered writings.[26]

A disciple, not a teacher

The two church orders are closest to the thought of the church fathers. Mary Magdalene is called a disciple without further ado.[27] It is assumed from this that as such she was also present at the Last Supper. However, according to the apostles that does not mean that women can play a role in the celebration of the eucharist. The Catholic Teaching of the Twelve Apostles mentions how the apostles discuss this subject among themselves. Martha and Mary Magdalene are present. Martha says that Jesus did not invite Mary to be present at the Last Supper because Mary laughed, not as a matter of principle. Mary emphasizes that she did not laugh about the Last Supper but because of the content of Jesus' teaching: 'the weak shall heal through the strong'. Martha's remark and Mary's retort are not accepted. Nevertheless the apostles conclude that it cannot have been Jesus' intention for women to administer the eucharist. It is not for women to serve the church; they are there to support those in need of help.[28]

In the Apostolic Church Order, the apostles defend the

diaconate of women with a reference to Mary Magdalene and the other women who served Jesus.[29] They also mention Mary Magdalene without any resevations as the first witness to the resurrection.[30] However, women cannot give instruction about this. The apostles say:

> It is neither right nor necessary for women to be teachers above all of the name of Christ and redemption through his suffering. For you are not appointed, women and above all widows, to give instruction but to pray and implore the Lord God. For the Lord God, Jesus Christ, our teacher, sent out us, the Twelve, to teach the peoples and the Gentiles; and there were women disciples among us, Mary Magdalene and Mary of James and the other Mary; but he did not sent them out with us to teach the people. For were it required that women should give teaching, then the master himself would have appointed them to teach alongside us (Apostolic Church Order III.6).

The two church orders do portray Mary Magdalene as a disciple, and that discipleship also leads to a function for women within the church (namely that of deacon). However, this function is clearly of a different order from that of the twelve male disciples. The women are asked to pray and to support those in need of help, while the men give instruction and are ministers at the eucharist.

Helper of Philip

In the Acts of Philip Jesus gives the mission command only to men, as the Apostolic Church Order presupposes. However, an exception is made for Mary Magdalene. She may go with Philip as a sister, to encourage him. When he had heard the name of the country and the city in which he had to proclaim the gospel, he had burst into tears. Mary, who, according to the Acts of Philip, kept the register of the lands to which the apostles went, then put in a good word for him with the Saviour. The Saviour answers as follows:

> I know that you are good and brave and that your soul is blessed among women. Behold Philip, the mind of a woman

has befallen him, whereas in you a manly and brave mind dwells (Acts of Philip 77).[31]

Then he gives her the task of joining Philip on his journey. But not as a woman. Christ says:

> As for you, Mary, change your clothing and your outward appearance: reject everything which from the outside suggests a woman (Acts of Philip 77).

And indeed she goes on the journey dressed in the monastic habit of a man. In the Acts of Philip, Mary is praised for her manliness and her asceticism. Although she is with Philip only to encourage him, she also preaches and baptizes. This then applies to women and not to men.[32]

A disciple: teaching and interpreting

The other writings are quite different in tone. They are also different kinds of works, more comparable to the New Testament Gospels than to the writings of the church fathers. The Gospel of Thomas and the Gospel of Philip contain wisdom sayings by Jesus and brief meditative texts. The Gospel of Peter and the Letter of the Apostles give an account of the resurrection. The other writings contain conversations between Jesus (before and after his resurrection, cf. Acts 1.3) and his disciples. In these writings, as in the church fathers, Mary Magdalene is firmly called a disciple. However, this is not in a restrictive sense, as it is in the later church fathers, the two church orders and the Acts of Philip. It does not mean that she is a disciple but not an apostle in the general meaning of the word nor a teacher, except as a helper, and disguised as a man and then only in connection with women. There is no mention in these writings of the limits of female discipleship. James says in the First Apocalypse of James:

> Yet another thing I ask of you: who are the seven women who have been your disciples? And behold all women bless you. I am also amazed how powerless vessels have become strong by a perception which is in them (First Apocalypse of James, 38).

According to James, the women disciples are above an occasion for all women to bless the Lord. In the manuscript it is difficult to read precisely what the answer is. It does, however, seem clear that it is meant to encourage Salome, Mary Magdalene, Martha and Arsinoe. That is what almost all the writings mentioned here show: the women disciples are encouraged rather than held back.

It is not surprising that we also find Mary Magdalene and other women as fully disciples and teachers, in contrast to the situation in the church fathers and the New Testament (with the exception of the Gospel of John). Like the other disciples, Mary Magdalene asks the Teacher questions and receives answers. In Pistis Sophia she asks by far the most questions.[33] A characteristic remark is:

> I do not get tired of asking you questions. Do not be cross because I ask you everything (Pistis Sophia 139).

Jesus' answer is an invitation: 'Ask what you will.' In the other writings Mary asks only a few questions, but they are very fundamental ones. Both in the Gospel of Thomas and in the Wisdom of Jesus Christ she asks about the nature and purpose of discipleship.[34] In the Wisdom of Jesus Christ she is the only one of the seven women to speak. Here she also asks how the disciples can come to know what they must know, the question of the source of knowledge of God.[35] In the Dialogue of the Saviour, along with Matthew and Judas she is one of the three disciples who receive special instruction. She asks about the meaning of sorrow and joy.[36] She also asks her brothers where and how they will keep all the things that the Lord tells them.[37]

Mary Magdalene not only asks questions but interprets. She has a good knowledge of scripture and of the sayings of Jesus. She searches out their meaning independently. In the Pistis Sophia she quotes Isaiah and the Psalms. She memorizes what Jesus says.[38] She also quotes wisdom sayings of Jesus in the Dialogue of the Saviour.[39] The author adds: 'She uttered this as a woman who had understood completely.' Mary Magdalene's insight is very highly esteemed.

A great insight

The narrator of the Dialogue of the Saviour is not the only one to portray Mary Magdalene as someone who has great insight into the divine. In Pistis Sophia she is repeatedly praised by the Lord himself. Her heart is said to be more attuned to the kingdom of heaven than those of any of her brothers.[40] She is to be praised above all women.[41] She puts the right questions accurately and purposefully.[42] In the kingdom of heaven, like John she will prove to be more acute than all the other disciples.[43]

In the Gospel of Philip the author relates that Christ loved Mary Magdalene more than all his disciples. When the disciples ask why this is so, the Lord replies:

> Why do I not love you like her? If a blind man and one who sees are both together in the darkness, they are no different from one another. When the light comes, then he who sees will see the light, and the blind will remain in darkness (Gospel of Philip 64.1–10).

Thus Mary Magdalene is compared with someone who sees. She can see the light. In the earthly night there is no difference between the disciples, but the coming of the light shows that there is. There are those who see and those who are blind.

The hostility of Peter

The question about Mary Magdalene in the Dialogue of the Saviour seems to conceal considerable annoyance about her position. In other writings it is Peter in particular who shows hostility. In the Gospel of Thomas he says:

> Let Mary leave us, for women are not worthy of life (Logion 114).

In the Gospel of Mary it is also Peter who turns against Mary.

This is a theme which still appears in the third century. In Pistis Sophia, Mary Magdalene says:

> My Lord, you always grasp my understanding, but each time I come forward to give the correct interpretation of your words I am afraid of Peter, for he threatens me and hates our sex (Pistis Sophia 72).

Earlier, Peter had said:

> My Lord, we cannot tolerate this woman any more: she does not allow any of us to say a word, whereas she speaks often (Pistis Sophia 36).

Both times the answer is that it is a matter of the person in whom the Spirit bubbles up. The Spirit speaks in Mary just as much as in Peter. Mary Magdalene is assured:

> Anyone who is filled with the spirit of life will come forward and expound what I say: no one shall be in a position to oppose them (Pistis Sophia 72).

This sounds very different from what the church father Origen envisaged in the same century. In commenting on Paul's First Letter to the Corinthians, he says:

> 'for it is shameful for a woman to speak in the community' (14.35b), whatever she says, even if she says admirable or holy things – as long as it comes out of the mouth of a woman.[44]

That Peter's hostility in Pistis Sophia is not directed against women in general is evident when Jesus tests his mercy. Jesus asks him to exclude from the kingdom of light a woman who has already been baptized three times but has never lived by her baptism. In response, Peter pleads with Jesus to give her one last chance. Moreover he will not take the final decision himself, but leaves it to Jesus.[45]

Jesus and Mary Magdalene: intimacy

Whereas the later church fathers and the two church orders emphasize the distance between Mary Magdalene and Jesus, the other writings show the intimacy between them.

This already begins in the Letter of the Apostles. As in the Gospel of Luke, the women's story about the resurrection is not believed. However, in contrast to Luke, they have been given the command to speak by the Lord himself. He has Mary Magdalene and Mary the sister of Martha going one by one. When they are still not believed, the Lord appears to the eleven disciples. However, he is not alone but takes the two Marys with him. They go together.[46] So with his solidarity the Lord shows that they are right. In the Gospel of Thomas, Jesus promises to give Mary Magdalene special guidance. In answer to Peter's request to exclude her from the circle of the disciples he says:

> I myself shall lead her in order to make her male, so that she too may become a living spirit resembling you males. For every woman who will make herself male will enter the kingdom of heaven (Gospel of Thomas, Logion 114).

The Gospel of Philip says that Mary Magdalene was called the companion of Jesus. Together with Mary the mother of Jesus and her sister she was always with him.[47] The author writes:

> The Saviour loved Mary Magdalene more than all the disciples, and kissed on her mouth often (Gospel of Philip 63.34–35)

We must not understand this 'kissing' in a sexual sense, but in a spiritual sense. The grace which those who kiss exchange makes them born again. This is already described earlier in the Gospel:

> If the children of Adam are numerous, although they die, how much more the children of the perfect man, who do not die but are continually born anew . . . They receive nourishment from the promise, to enter into the place above. The promise comes from the mouth, for the Word has come from there and has been nourished from the mouth and become perfect. The perfect conceive through a kiss and give birth. Because of this we also kiss one another. We receive conception from the grace which we have among us (Gospel of Philip 58.20–59.6).

Mary Magdalene is made fruitful through the grace which is in Christ. Receiving his grace makes her born again.

The distance between Jesus and Mary Magdalene in the later church fathers is a distance between the sinful woman and God. The intimacy shown by the writings mentioned here is the intimacy of teacher and pupil.

The fetter of oblivion

'The fetter of oblivion is temporal' says the Gospel of Mary. This sentence keeps occurring to me when I realize how much more we now know of the earliest traditions about Mary Magdalene than we did two centuries ago. At that time we would have had to be content with the texts preserved by the church tradition. Now, thanks to the new discoveries, we have an impression of the breadth of the early Christian church. In a number of recently discovered writings Mary Magdalene is a disciple in the full sense of the word. There are discussions with Jesus about his teaching in which she puts questions just like the other disciples and interprets his words as one who knows scripture well. She is depicted as a person with great insight and an intense spiritual relationship with Jesus.

The fetter of oblivion is temporal. Until around 200 years ago, Mary Magdalene was trapped in the picture that church tradition had preserved from antiquity. Up to the fourth century, that picture is one of the pious helper and obedient believer; it is the picture that takes up the Gospel of Matthew and the Gospel of Luke. The myth has now been broken by the discoveries in the desert. In antiquity there also seems to have been another picture of Mary Magalene, the picture of the disciple on the same footing as Peter, the picture of the disciple with a special insight. It is a picture which follows more the line of the Gospel of Mark and the Gospel of John.

The ambivalence which was already detectable above all in Matthew and Luke continued in church tradition. Certainly Mary Magdalene is a disciple, and according to church tradition she can even call herself apostle, but then come the ifs and buts. The catalyst which Mary Magdalene is in Mark and John seemed to have been passed over. Now we know better. That is our great gain from what the desert sands have yielded.

New discoveries, new questions

However, the new discoveries also raise new questions.

The recently discovered writings certainly do not contain ideas which later became current in the church. The writings which give Mary Magdalene rather more of a role are in general attributed to a spiritual tendency which the church of the third century and later doggedly opposed: Christian Gnosticism. I shall be saying more about that in the next chapter.

That makes the second question in our search for Mary Magdalene – the question to which so far we have hardly found an answer – all the more pressing. What is Mary Magdalene's story? What did she have to tell, that she could be ranked so highly by Gnosticism?

Our first question also comes to stand in another light. Who was she? What led to her being mentioned with so much respect in the second and third centuries? Did she have followers?

And then there is the hostile attitude of Peter, an attitude which picks up what we already found in the Gospel of Luke and the Gospel of John. Was there rivalry between Peter and Mary Magdalene or between their followers? And if that was the case, what was the reason for it?

In the next chapter we shall see whether the Gospel of Mary can help us further.

4

The Gospel of Mary

'Mariam, Mariam, know me: do not touch me.
Stem the tears of thy eyes
and know me that I am thy master . . .
Cast this sadness away from thee
and do this service:
be a messenger for me to these wandering orphans.
Use all skill and advice
until thou hast brought the sheep to the shepherd.'
'Rabbi, my master,
I will serve thy commandment
in the joy of my whole heart.
I will not give rest to my heart,
I will not give sleep to my eyes,
I will not give rest to my feet
until I have brought the sheep to the fold.'
Glory to Mary,
because she hearkened to her master.
She served his commandment
in the joy of her whole heart.

(Psalm of Heraclides 1, 2–5, 22–23, 30–32).

The Gospel of Mary. That sounds different from the Gospel of Matthew, of Luke, of John, of Thomas, or of Peter. When one looks at the Gospels that we have, one keeps coming across men's names. That's logical, we say. That's how it was at that time. Men had the last word. The Gospel of Mary allows another voice to be heard. In this Gospel a woman is speaking with authority about the things of the Lord: Mary Magdalene. She puts the confused disciples on the track of the Teacher again.

Preface

Discovery and publication

Cairo 1896. The German scholar C.Reinhardt is wandering through the city, trying his luck with more or less trustworthy antique dealers. He will not be the first person to come upon valuable items in this way. In one of the shops he is offered a bundle of papyri, papyri sheets in book form. The manuscript is in Coptic, the last phase of Old Egyptian, in which Greek words also appear. From the numbering of the pages it can be seen that the codex is not complete. But the quality is good and so is the content. The codex contains four writings: the Gospel of Mary, the Apocryphon of John, the Wisdom of Jesus Christ and the Acts of Peter.

Reinhard senses the value of the papyri and makes an offer.

The antique dealer can tell him little about the original discovery. He bought the codex from a colleague in Akhmim. This colleague could tell him that the codex, wrapped in feathers, was discovered in a niche in a wall in a burial place near Akhmim.

The discovery was brought to Berlin and is in the Egyptology Department of the National Museum under the name Papyrus Berolinensis 8502.[1]

There the codex, now the Berlin Codex, patiently awaits its further fate.

Ouderkerk aan de Amstel 1996. A century later. The discovery of the Gospel of Mary is, at least in wider circles, still as unknown as in 1896. Why?

The history of its publication is in any case a sad one. The famous Coptic scholar C.Schmidt had already announced the discovery of the papyrus in 1896. In 1912 he had worked on the text enough for it to be published. However, a flood at the printers in Leipzig destroyed the proofs. Shortly before his death in 1938, Schmidt revised the work. The Coptic scholar W.C.Till was able to work on it between 1941 and 1943, but it was not possible to publish it during the Second World War. Subsequently there was the discovery at Nag Hammadi, two manuscripts of which seemed to be important for the publication of the papyrus from the Berlin Codex. All in all, the text of Papyrus Berolinensis

8502 was not published until 1955, almost sixty years after the date its existence was first announced. Till produced a translation and a short commentary.[2] For a long time there was no scholarly interest, and even now scholars are not very impressed.

It was a piece of luck that the Nag Hammadi library contained two writings which were also in the Berlin Codex: the Apocryphon of John and the Wisdom of Jesus Christ. Moreover when the Nag Hammadi library appeared in an English translation in 1977, the editor decided also to include the two other texts from the Berlin Papyrus, the Gospel of Mary and the Acts of Peter.[3] That made the Gospel of Mary better known.

In 1983 the first extended commentary on the Gospel of Mary appeared. The Canadian scholar Anne Pasquier had been able to study the papyrus extensively. That led to a critical edition of the text. A translation and short commentary by G.P.Luttikhuizen appeared in the Netherlands in 1986.[4]

Dating

On the basis of a comparison of various manuscripts the famous papyrologist C.H.Roberts thinks that the original version of the Gospel of Mary must have already existed in the second half of the second century.[5] Therefore as the upper limit of the composition of the Gospel I have opted for 150.

Perhaps something could also be said about the lower limit. If we look at the content of the Gospel, it is striking that the Gospel of Mary has a number of marked agreements with the New Testament Gospels.[6] However, that need not mean that the Gospel of Mary must be later, i.e. 80 at the earliest. It could have drawn on the same earlier (unknown) sources as the New Testament Gospels.[7]

Another point of contact in the content relevant to the lower limit of dating is the discussion about the place of Mary which appears in the Gospel. Peter thinks that her witness is illegitimate. Surely the Saviour did not speak with a woman but with men, so why should they, men, have to listen to a woman?

This kind of discussion does not occur in the New Testament Gospels. We might possibly begin from the assumption that a public discussion about Mary Magdalene as a woman was already being carried on before the New Testament Gospels and, at least for the writers who later found a place in the Bible, was decided to the disadvantage of Mary. That would be an explanation of why so little attention has been paid to her in the New Testament and in the writings of the apostolic fathers. In that case we should put an early lower limit to the dating of the Gospel of Mary, even before the New Testament Gospels. However, I shall not do that. It is more probable that not having to listen to a woman only became a point of discussion from the end of the first century on.

Paul still speaks quite openly in his Letter to the Galatians about the belief that

> in Christ there is neither Jew nor Greek, there is neither slave nor free, there is neither male nor female (Gal.3.28).

This is a statement which is still very close to the remarkable teaching of Jesus. Social position, religious background and being male or female may be important in the eyes of human beings, but they are not in the sight of God, and therefore not in the community either. Around ten years later, in his First Letter to the Corinthians, Paul is more restrained. The subject-matter is the same: baptism. He mentions Jew and Greek, slave and free again, but omits male and female (I Cor.12.13). Paul introduces a hierarchical relationship: God is the head of Christ, Christ is the head of the man and the man is the head of the woman (I Cor.11.3). However, this hierarchy as yet has no consequences for an authoritative role of women in the community. Paul uses it to indicate that the man may not cover his head whenever he is praying or prophesying and the woman may not leave her head uncovered whenever she is praying or prophesying. Thus both men and women pray and prophesy. The prophetically gifted had great authority in the communities. Some scholars think that the much-quoted text from the same letter which tells women nevertheless to be silent in the community is a later addition (I Cor.14.33b–36).[8] In any case, Paul himself has connections with women who like him are committed to the spreading of the gospel. Here he mentions among others Prisca, Junia, Phoebe, Mary, Persis, Tryphena and Tryphosa, Euodia and Syntyche (Rom.16.1–16; Phil.4.2–3). He certainly does not tell them to be silent, even in the assemblies of the community, but praises them and their work highly.[9]

That something nevertheless is changing is evident from a comparison between the Gospel of Luke and the Gospel of John. Luke has clearly reflected on the role of women. He emphasizes that they were disciples of Jesus (Luke 8.1–3). By means of the story about Martha and Mary he encourages his woman readers also to become full disciples of Jesus: not only to serve Jesus but also to learn from him (Luke 10.38–42). But at the same time there is a qualification: women already follow Jesus by serving, learning and praying, but no independent task of proclamation is set apart for them (Luke 24.5–7; Acts 1.12–26).

In the Gospel of John there is the first trace of a discussion comparable to that initiated by Peter in the Gospel of Mary. When Jesus' disciples found him in the company of the Samaritan woman, they

> marvelled that he was talking with a woman, but none said, 'What do you wish?' or 'Why are you talking with her?' (John 4.27).

Evidently also according to this Gospel the disciples were surprised that Jesus was speaking alone with a woman, with no men present, but they understood that they must not intervene. In the Gospel of John, in contrast to Luke, the task of proclamation is indeed laid on women (John 4.39; 20.17–18).

How sharp the discussion became is evident from the First Letter to Timothy, in which a disciple of Paul refers his readers to Eve. She was the one who allowed herself to be led astray. Adam did not. So a woman must keep quiet, live modestly and bring children into the world. He writes:

> Let a woman learn in silence with all submissiveness. I permit no woman to teach or to have authority over men; she is to keep silent. For Adam was formed first, then Eve; and Adam was not deceived, but the woman was deceived and became a transgressor. Yet woman will be saved through bearing children, if she continues in faith and love and holiness, with modesty.

These words were written around 100.

In view of all this we may assume – in addition to the upper limit of 150 – that the lower limit of the dating of the Gospel of Mary is to be put not earlier than the end of the first century, i.e. round about the composition of the Gospel of John. The open discussion about the fact that Mary is a woman seems to point to that. So the Gospel would have been composed not later than 150 and not earlier than 90. Obviously such a dating is relative. Parts of the Gospel of Mary could go back to oral and written traditions older than the Gospel itself.

Origin and dissemination

All kinds of manuscripts have been discovered of the New Testament Gospels. If you set them in order, the result is a kind of history of the Gospels. Where were they all known? Where were they widely read?

We have three manuscripts of the Gospel of Mary, two in Greek from the third century and one in Coptic from the fifth century. The codex discovered by Reinhard was the one in Coptic from the fifth century.[10]

In 1938, C.H.Roberts discovered that a papyrus fragment from the Rylands collection also contained the Gospel of Mary, but in Greek. That fragment, which contains only a few verses of the Gospel of Mary (part of EvMar 10), comes from the beginning of the third century. It was also found in Egypt, in the ancient city of Oxyrhynchus (now Behnessa). A third Greek fragment of the Gospel of Mary came to light in 1985 (EvMar 17–19). That also comes from the third century, also from Oxyrhynchus.[11]

The Coptic manuscript is in the Sahidic dialect. That was the language generally used by Egyptians of that time. The two Greek manuscripts were found together with many other papyri, predominantly Greek and Latin. In the Roman and Byzantine periods, the city of Oxyrhynchus, where the discovery was made, was the chief city in Middle Egypt. The city also had a public library.[12] The papyri discovered come from the period between 250 BCE and the seventh century. They contain fragments of literary, historical, religious and popular writings and also fragments of letters and documents.[13]

So far, the fragments of religious literature found come from Genesis, Exodus, Leviticus, Joshua, Psalms, Job, Ecclesiastes and Amos; also from Tobit. There are fragments of all four New Testament Gospels, of Acts, Paul's Letter to the Romans, I Corinthians, Galatians, Philippians and I and II Thessalonians. There are also fragments of the letters of James, Peter and Jude, Hebrews, the letters of John, and Revelation. These are all writings which the later church put on the list of books which might be read. However, fragments have also been found of books which did not get on to this list, fragments of VI Ezra and the Apocalypse of Baruch, the Acts of Paul and Thecla, the Acts of Peter and the Acts of John, as also of the Shepherd of Hermas, the Gospel of Peter, the Protevangelium of James and the Wisdom of Jesus Christ. Sayings of Jesus have also been found which strongly suggest the Gospel of Thomas. All the writings from Oxyrhynchus mentioned above originated from outside Egypt. That makes it possible to assume that the Gospel of Mary, which was originally written in Greek, was also in fact composed outside Egypt.

It is striking that both Greek versions of the Gospel have been found so closely connected with writings which the church tradition later put on strictly separate lists of what was 'to be read' and 'not to be read'. This fact is silent testimony to the pluriformity of early Christianity. This is a pluriformity which, moreover, also found its limits before Oxyrhynchus. In almost all the Christian writings found there the first apostles play an important role. Moreover without exception they are to be dated early: in the first and second centuries. As far as Gnosticism is concerned, the really Gnostic names like Valentinus, Cerinthus, Basilides, Bardesanes and Mani are missing. The names of Marcion, who is akin to Gnosticism, and his disciple Apelles also do not occur.

The Coptic manuscript of the Gospel of Mary was found further north than Middle Egypt and moreover in a more Gnostic context. One of the four writings of the Berlin codex, the Apocryphon of John, is specifically Gnostic. Perhaps we may begin from the assumption that the Gospel of Mary was increasingly understood as a Gnostic writing.

At all events we can conclude that the Gospel of Mary was

thought sufficiently worth reading to be translated into the language of the ordinary Egyptian. Moreover the Gospel was also read in the north of Egypt until the fifth century and presumably even later, given the discovery in the nineteenth century.

Whether the Gospel was known even further north, and whether it also had a circle of readers outside Egypt, for example in Europe or Asia Minor, is not clear. It is possible, given that the Gospel was probably not written in Egypt. However, no manuscripts have been discovered outside Egypt, nor does any church father seem to be familiar with the Gospel.

The identity of Mary

Less than half of the Gospel of Mary has been preserved. Ten of the nineteen pages are missing. The remaining nine pages always speak of 'Mary' and never of 'Mary Magdalene'. However, it is thought that 'Mary' here means the Mary Magdalene of the Gospel. Mary Magdalene is in fact similarly called Mary in the same sort of writing as the Gospel of Mary; from this we may readily conclude that the Gospel of Mary is also about Mary Magdalene.

In the Gospel of Mary it is Peter who is opposed to what Mary says, because she is a woman. Peter has the same role in the Gospel of Thomas and Pistis Sophia. In both cases the Mary concerned is Mary Magdalene. The Gospel of Mary makes Levi say that the Redeemer loved Mary 'more than us' (EvMar 18.14–15). There is a comparable statement in the Gospel of Philip which also clearly refers to Mary Magdalene.[14]

Translation

Here is a translation of the Coptic text. The capitals have been added.[15] The page and line numbers are those of the manuscript.
    (pp. 1–6 are missing)

[7]
. . . will matter then be destroyed or not?
The Saviour said,
'All Nature, all formations, all creations
exist in and with one another,

5 and they will be dissolved again into their own roots.
For the Nature of matter is dissolved
into the things that belong to its Nature alone.
He who has ears to hear, let him hear.'
10 Peter said to him, 'Since you have told us all things,
tell us this also: What is the sin of the world?'
The Saviour said,
'There is no sin, but it is you who do sin
15 when you do the things
which accord with the nature of adultery,
that is called sin.
That is why the Good came into your midst,
to those who belong to all Nature,
in order to restore it to its root.'
20 Then he continued and said,
'That is why you are sick and die, for . . .

[8]   •
[He who] understands, let him understand.
[Matter gave birth to suffering]
that has no model, because it proceeded from an opposite
nature.
5 Since then there has been confusion in the whole body.
That is why I said to you,
'Be of one heart and be without mixing
because you are one
in respect of the different aspects of nature.
10 He who has ears to hear, let him hear,'
When the Blessed One had said these things,
he embraced them all, saying,
'Peace be with you. Bring forth my peace from yourselves.
15 Beware that no one lead you astray,
saying, "Lo here!" or "Lo there!"
For the Human One is within you.
20 Follow after him Those who seek him will find him.
Go then and preach the gospel of the kingdom.

[9]
Do not lay down any other rules than those I appointed for you,

and do not give a law like the lawgiver
so that you are not being held prisoner by it.'
5 When he had said these things, he departed.
But they were grieved and wept greatly,
saying,
'How shall we go to the nations and preach the gospel of the
kingdom of the Human One?
10 If they did not spare him, how will they spare us?'
Then Mary stood up, embraced them all, and said to her
brothers,
15 'Do not weep and do not grieve and do not make two hearts,
for his grace will be with you all
and will protect you.
Rather let us praise his greatness,
because he has prepared us.
20 He has made us Human Being.
When Mary had said these things,
she turned their hearts inwards, to the Good,
and they began to practise the words of the [Saviour].

[10]
Peter said to Mary,
'Sister, we know that the Saviour loved you more
than the rest of the women.
Tell us the words of the Saviour which you remember
5 the things that you know and we do not,
nor have we heard them.'
Mary answered, she said,
'What is hidden from you I shall tell you.'
And she began to say to them these words:
10 'I,' she said, 'I saw the Lord in a vision and I said to him,
"Lord, I saw you today in a vision."
He answered, he said to me,
"Blessed are you, because you are not shaken
15 when you see me.
For where the mind (*nous*) is,
there is the treasure."
I said to him, "Lord, now, does he who sees the vision
see it with the soul (*psyche*)

or with the spirit (*pneuma*)?
The Saviour answered, he said,
20 'He does not see with the soul nor with the spirit,
but with the mind which [is] between the two
that is [what] sees the vision and that is . . .'

(pp.11–14 are missing)

[15]
him and Desire said:
'I did not see you, when you were on the way to earth,
but now I see you, while you are on the way to heaven.
How can you deceive me, when you belong to me?'
5 The soul answered and said,
'I saw you. You did not see me
nor recognize me.
I served you as a garment, and you did not know me.'
When it had said these things, it went away rejoicing loudly.
10 Again it came to the third power,
which is called Ignorance.
[It] questioned the soul, saying,
'Where are you going?
By wickedness you are held prisoner.
15 Yes, you are held. Do not judge!'
And the soul said,
'Why do you judge me although I have not judged?
I am held prisoner
because I have not held prisoner.
20 I am not recognized, but I have recognized
that the All is being dissolved,
both the earthly things and the heavenly things.

[16]
When the soul had freed itself from the third power,
it went upwards and saw the fourth power.
This took seven forms.
5 The first form is Darkness, the second Desire, the third
Ignorance, the fourth is the Jealousy of Death, the fifth is the
Kingdom of the Flesh,

the sixth is the Foolish Learning of Flesh,
the seventh is the Hot-Tempered Wisdom.
These are the seven [power]s of Wrath.
They ask the soul,
15 'Where do you come from, you slayer of men?',
or, 'Where are you going, you who free yourself from places?'
The soul answered, it said,
'He who holds me prisoner is pierced.
I am free of him who turns me about
20 And my desire has been completed,
and ignorance has died.
From a world I am released through a world,

[17]
and from a model through a model which is from the side of
heaven.
And the fetter of oblivion is temporal.
5 From this hour on I shall receive the rest
– at the time, of the decisive moment in the aeon –
in silence.'
When Mary had said these things, she shut her mouth,
because it was to this point that the Saviour had spoken with
her.
10 Now Andrew answered and said to the brothers,
'Tell me, what do you (wish to) say about the things that she
has spoken?
I at least do not believe
that the Saviour said these things.
15 For these teachings
seem to be strange ideas.'
Peter answered, he spoke about these same things.
He reflected about the Saviour:
'Surely he did not speak with a woman
20 without our knowledge and not openly?
Are we to turn about and all listen to her? Has
he chosen her above us?'

[18]
Then Mary wept, she said to Peter,

'My brother Peter, what are you thinking?
Do you suppose that I devised this, alone, in my heart,
5 or that I am deceiving the Saviour?'
Levi answered and said to Peter,
'Peter, you have always been hot-tempered.
Now I see you arguing with the woman
like these adversaries.
10 If the Saviour has made her worthy,
who are you indeed to reject her?
Surely the Saviour knows her very well.
That is why he loved her more than us.
15 Rather let us be ashamed
and put on the perfect Human Being.
Let us bring him forth from ourselves.
as he commanded us.
Let us preach the gospel,
without laying down any other rule
20 or another law than what the Saviour said.'

[19]
When Levi had said these things, they began to go forth to
proclaim and to preach.
The Gospel
according to
Mary

Construction and message

A first acquaintance with the Gospel of Mary can be disappoint-
ing. What can one make of a Gospel more than half of which is
missing? What does one do with comments about nature and
matter and powers which try to keep the soul from heavenly rest?
What does one do with a weeping Mary who defends herself only
minimally from Peter and Andrew?

Yet the Gospel of Mary has occupied me for years. That is
especially because of the passage shortly after the departure of the
Saviour, the part in the middle of the Gospel. There the disciples
ask:

How shall we go to the nations and preach the gospel of the

kingdom of the Human One? If they did not spare him, how will they spare us? (EvMar 9.7–12)

It is a penetrating and desperate question.

Mary's answer has gripped me from the first time that I read it. She takes the question quite seriously. She does not trivialize the anxiety. She does not give any false hope. She simply says,

He has prepared us, he has made us Human Being (EvMar 9.19–20).

Another passage which I find intriguing is Peter's question, which is certainly not well-disposed towards women, and the straight answer that Levi gives to it:

But if the Saviour made her worthy, who are you indeed to reject her? (EvMar 18.10–12).

Three ways of reading

The first commentary on the Gospel of Mary appeared in 1983. It was a doctoral thesis by the Canadian Anne Pasquier. Soon afterwards, in 1984, the Frenchman Michel Tardieu wrote a commentary, not only on the Gospel but on the whole of the Berlin Codex.[16] The first editor, the Austrian Walter Till, had already produced a translation of the text with a short introduction in 1955. More has been written on the Gospel, but I simply want to present the views of these three authors, because each of them has an original approach. Till's insights are often quoted. Those of Pasquier and Tardieu are less well-known. Each of the three has quite a different view of the construction of the Gospel of Mary. This has consequences for how each of them thinks of the message of the Gospel.

Till's starting point is that the Gospel of Mary as it was found originally consisted of two writings which have been rather clumsily put together. The Saviour plays the main role in the first work and Mary in the second. Till sees the link between the two in the weeping disciples who have been left behind, and Mary's words of comfort to them. In his judgment, the Gospel of Mary proper begins only where Peter asks Mary to relate the teaching which the Saviour has given to her and not to others (EvMar 10.1).

According to Till, the purpose of the Gospel is to depict Mary Magdalene, the first witness of the resurrection, as a proclaimer of Gnostic teaching. Her insight is clearly superior to that of the apostles. Moreover Till points out that the Gnostic teaching of the Gospel of Mary is not secret, as is usually the case in the other Gnostic writings. The Gospel of Mary speaks about the proclamation without remarking that it is meant only for those who are ripe for it.

Pasquier, too, speaks of two writings which have been woven together, but in a different way from Till. Her view is influenced by the strange way in which Peter contradicts himself. First he lets Mary speak because she knows more than the brothers. Later he questions precisely that. Suddenly he seems no longer able to imagine how the Saviour could have spoken only with Mary without the others being present.

This leads Pasquier to the following hypothesis. The whole passage from Peter's question about Mary's recollections up to or including Andrew's reaction (EvMar 9.21–17.9/15) was not originally part of the Gospel. The conversation between the Saviour and Mary about visions and about the journey of the soul thus drops out. Peter's malicious comment is then not about this account but about Mary's words when she addresses the weeping disciples. He objects above all to the word 'us' in the sentence 'He has made us Human Being' (EvMar 9.20). According to Peter, Mary is not Human Being but a woman.

In Pasquier's view, Peter thus represents the orthodox thinking of the second century, that the appearances of the risen Christ to women did not in themselves give them the right to preach the message of the resurrection, far less exercise authority over the Christian community.

By contrast, the Gospel of Mary allows us to hear an unorthodox voice. Peter is portrayed as an opponent. His view of women runs contrary to that of the Saviour. According to Pasquier, the Gospel shows that Mary can take preaching upon herself because only she has already really become Human Being. She has achieved the androgynous unity which the disciples still lack. It is the purpose of the Gospel to use such

Gnostic arguments in the struggle against orthodoxy. Women, too, can exercise authority in the Christian community.

Tardieu regards the Gospel of Mary, in the form in which it was discovered, as a unity. In his view, neither form nor content gives us any reason to assume that two different writings lie behind the Coptic manuscript. He agrees with Till that the text consists of two parts, but these belong indissolubly together. Their aim is to emphasize the pre-eminent place of Mary Magdalene. In the second part she takes over the main role that the Saviour had in the first part. Nor do the subjects discussed suggest that one of the two parts was added later. There is a clear development in their order. We have the Creator and his creation, sin and its consequences, salvation through gnosis and the journey of the soul after death. Thus the Gospel of Mary offers a short survey of the essential doctrines of Gnosticism.

Gnosticism

Till, Pasquier and Tardieu each have very distinct insights into the message of the Gospel of Mary. The differences in interpretation are to be derived from different presuppositions about the structure of the Gospel. Till thinks that only the second part of the Coptic manuscript contains the Gospel of Mary. According to Pasquier, the middle does not belong, and Tardieu presupposes that the manuscript and the Gospel are identical.

However, the three scholars are agreed on one thing. The Gospel of Mary is about gnosis.

Gnosis is a Greek word which literally means 'knowledge', 'insight'. This is not scientific knowledge but knowledge gained through revelation. The church father Clement of Alexandria cites the Gnostic Theodotus (second century) when he says that Gnosticism is about the

knowledge of who we were and what we have become, of where we were and into what we are thrown, where we are going and from what we are redeemed, what is birth and what is rebirth (*Excerpta ex Theodoto* 78.2).

Gnostics are convinced that they do not belong on this earth. They are like gold on a dungheap. They are strangers on earth, for they belong to God, to the spiritual world. By an unfortunate chance they are trapped in matter, in the material world, but they will be able to return to the spiritual world through insight into their situation.[17]

The Gospel of Mary is categorized as Gnostic dialogue. On the basis of thirteen works which belong to that genre, Pheme Perkins arrived at the following description.[18]

Gnostic dialogue consists of a revelation discourse framed by narrative elements. In the introduction the narrator speaks in general terms about the place of revelation (often a mountain, e.g. the Mount of Olives), the time (usually after the resurrection) and the recipients (in almost all cases these are names known from the New Testament). The Saviour appears to them at the moment when they are persecuted, proclaim the gospel or reflect on Jesus' words. They are anxious, sorrowful and confused, or sunk in prayer. The Saviour introduces himself with 'I am' sayings, makes clear the purpose of his coming and rebukes the disciples for their unbelief.

Then follows the revelation discourse proper, through questions put by the disciples. The content of the proclamation is often information about the origin of the cosmos, redemption and the true (i.e. Gnostic) Christian teaching: for example about baptism, the crucifixion and the interpretation of the scriptures (usually the New Testament). By far the greatest part of the revelation discourses concentrates on questions about redemption.

At the end the disciples are given the task of handing on what they have been told to those who are worthy, or of protecting the revelation against those who dispute it. Their reaction is one of gratitude and joy.

In the Gnostic world the creator is seen as a lower deity. The true God is radically transcendent. He has nothing to do with this ungodly world, except with human beings. They are bound to him in their deepest selves, but they have forgotten this. It is the task of the Saviour to remind human beings of their bond with God and thus of their true identity. Moreover he has to overcome the demonic powers which keep human beings imprisoned in this cosmos. For a Gnostic believer, the complete realization of redemption consists in the return to God after death (the journey of the soul). Already in this life believers must strive to get free of matter and its passions by an ascetic life-style. Perkins comments that the ideas about redemption in Gnostic dialogues differ hardly, if at all, from the pluriform Christian views of the second century, though they do so in the third century and later. However, the conviction that God is radically transcendent and has nothing to do with the cosmos stands in strong contrast to the views of the divine which are characteristic of the second century.

Like Perkins, Till, Pasquier and Tardieu presuppose that the radical transcendence of God and the rejection of matter underlie the Gospel of Mary.

Tardieu also thinks that the Gospel presents Gnostic teaching attractively and simply. That is also why, he says, it is the first writing in the Berlin Codex. It serves as an introduction. Tardieu supposes that the Saviour on pp.1–6 has explained that the true God is not the same as the creator of heaven and earth. From p.7 on he interprets the Gospel of Mary as follows.

Human beings must rise above the cycle of nature by escaping from it. To achieve this it is necessary to refrain from procreation. Sexuality is the great sin. Passion, desire lies at the root of all suffering. Mary adds that it is the *nous* that can bring order to the turbulence of the soul. Direct contact with the Saviour is possible through the *nous*. After death this same *nous* can convince the powers which control the world of their ignorance and thus of their impotence.

Pasquier sees the gnosis of the Gospel above all in the notion of androgyny. A frequent symbol in Gnosticism is that of the wedding. The soul has landed on earth because part of God, namely Wisdom, turned her back on her male partner. She wanted to be independent and to be able to act autonomously. According to Pasquier, this whole myth underlies the Gospel of Mary. Thus she does not just interpret the word adultery literally, as Tardieu does, but also figuratively. Wisdom has committed adultery and that is how all wretchedness began. She is the reason why heaven and earth came into being alongside the divine world. Christ was sent to earth to show the way back, to reunite each soul with its male element. The soul must be complete again. That is why the Gospel of Mary, too, speaks of a perfect Human Being. When the work of redemption is done, heaven and earth will disappear.

Finally, Till describes the gnosis which the Gospel of Mary seeks to convey. Above all he investigates the journey of the soul.

In his view, in the end this account forms the greatest part of the Gospel. For him, the four powers which hold back the soul on its journey to the world are the four elements: earth, water, air and fire. They are indicated by the names Darkness, Desire, Ignorance and Wrath. Each power wants to hold the soul in its grasp by discouraging it. What Darkness says is no longer extant. Desire tries to dissuade the soul from being parted from the divine world. It is earthly through and through, and thus must bow to the earthly powers. Ignorance points out that the soul cannot reach the divine world because it is a captive in its material body. Wrath puts the whole phenomenon of gnosis in doubt with the questions: 'Where do you think you come from? And where do you think you are going?' By remaining true to the Gnostic teaching, the soul can achieve the divine world of rest and silence, despite the fierce opposition of the four powers.

To sum up: the three most important scholarly investigations into the Gospel of Mary have different presuppositions, but agree that the Gospel is about gnosis. How the Gospel speaks of this, and on what elements of Gnostic thought it draws, are again questions the answer to which depends on the presuppositions. Tardieu assumes that the whole of Gnostic teaching is being presented in a simple and attractive way. Pasquier thinks that the Gospel of Mary has to do above all with the notion of androgyny, and according to Till the salvation of the soul after death is central.

To avoid confusing terminology it is important for us to realize that the modern use of the word 'gnosis' only in part links up with its usage in antiquity. The specific characteristic of ancient gnosis is radical dualism, hostility towards matter. Modern gnosis is characterized by the notion of holism: everything is connected with everything else and there is ultimately harmony. Since the Gospel of Mary is a writing from antiquity and our quest for Mary Magdalene is also limited to antiquity, in this book I use gnosis in its classical sense.

Give room to the text

Three scholarly investigations: three different interpretations of the Gospel of Mary.

In 1985 I went to the conference on 'Images of the Feminine in Gnosticism' which was organized by the Institute for Antiquity and Christianity based at Claremont and by the Society of Biblical Literature.[19] It was the first conference on this topic, and discussions were vigorous. There, too, one could hear very different interpretations of the same texts.

I remember one contribution in particular. During the evaluation of the conference one of the speakers, Frederik Wisse, emphasized that texts, and certainly ancient texts, are vulnerable. A text cannot fight back, he said. Exegetes must above all aim to give room to the text which is to be interpreted. Extra care is needed when the texts have a mystical (or mythological) aspect.

Give the text as much room as possible. At first sight that advice seems to be a matter of course. But this starting point has led me to other presuppositions than those underlying the three interpretations given above.

I assume that the structure of the Gospel of Mary as we now have it is coherent unless the text itself convincingly shows otherwise.

I would put the content of the Gospel in the context of the pluriform Christian spirituality, not yet crystallized into dogma, which was so distinctive of the Christian faith of the first and second centuries of our era. So my starting point is not that the message of the Gospel of Mary is specifically Gnostic, although the Gospel displays unmistakable elements which could be interpreted in terms of Gnosticism. However, I do not presuppose that God is radically transcended, that matter is reprehensible and the creator is a lower deity – in contrast to the Jewish, Christian and philosophical views of the divine characteristic of the first and second centuries. If the Gospel wanted to present this view, that should be convincingly evident from the text itself. And by that I mean the text as it has been found.

Till distinguishes two writings, one in which the Saviour plays the chief role and one in which Mary is the prominent figure. He concludes from this that the Gospel of Mary begins at 10.1. However, the text does not compel us to presuppose this, at least until the first pages of the Gospel of Mary are found. It may well be that Mary also speaks in the first six pages of the Gospel.

Till presupposes that EvMar 9.5–23 is a passage added later

which holds the two writings together artificially. However, the text as found shows a high degree of cohesion. The intermediate passage refers back to the first part. The suffering, the being of one heart, the assurance that the disciples have the Human One within them, i.e. much of what appears on p.9, is prepared for on p.8. Moreover the second part is connected with the beginning. The dissolution of the All, a Human Being, Jesus' counsels – the same subjects appear both on pp.7 and 8 and on pp.15 and 18. Here the second part sometimes refers back to the interim passage. The words of Mary on p.9 can be heard in the words of Levi on p.18.

Pasquier's hypothesis that 9.21–17.9/15 did not originally belong to the Gospel of Mary rests on the fact that Peter contradicts himself in an unmistakable way. First he says:

> Tell us the words of the Saviour which you remember, the things that you know and we do not, nor have we heard them (10.5–6).

Later he cannot imagine how Mary as a woman can know more than the men:

> Surely he did not speak with a woman without our knowledge and not openly? Are we to turn about and all listen to her? Has he chosen her above us? (EvMar 17.18–22).

According to Pasquier, Peter's words in 17.18–22 take up Mary's remarks in 9.20 without a break. The Gospel of Mary is more coherent without 9.21–17.9/15 than with it.

Anyone who wants to give the text a chance must take into account the possibility that the author of the Gospel of Mary is deliberately emphasizing Peter's inconsistency. It may be that his changing attitude is meant to demonstrate something.

The key to Peter's behaviour, which is at first sight inexplicable, lies in the answer given to him by Levi. Levi says:

> Peter, you have always been hot-tempered. Now I see you arguing with the woman like these adversaries (EvMar 18.7–10).

We can make out from Levi's answer that it is Peter's temper which underlies his intrinsically inconsistent behaviour.

But that is not all. Levi says more. His answer reveals the identity of the adversaries. They are the powers of Darkness, Desire, Ignorance and Wrath.[20] They bring their arguments to bear in order to deter the soul from its way to the Rest. Levi's comparison of Peter with 'these adversaries' is incomplete. Within the direct context, the comparison can only be filled in as follows:

> Now I see you arguing with the woman like these adversaries *arguing with the soul.*

Here Levi is giving his view of the nature of the temper which holds Peter in its grip. The seventh form of the fourth power, the Hot-Tempered Wisdom, is holding Peter in its grip (EvMar 16.11). That means that Levi, unlike Andrew and Peter, takes Mary's contribution quite seriously and himself follows it. He sees the force of the Powers which she describes demonstrated in Peter. The Powers are strong. They can get a grip even on the disciples of the Lord, and even when they are occupied with the things of the Lord (9.22f.). Andrew also brings Mary into discredit by stubbornly asserting that he does not believe that her words come from the Saviour. He comes to this far-reaching conclusion on the basis of an argument which according to him apparently needs no further explanation. He just says:

> For these teachings seem to be strange ideas (EvMar 17.14–15).

He tests Mary's words by what he and the brothers already know from the Saviour. Mary, who can lift the weeping brothers out of their sorrow, cannot now hold back her own tears.

With their reaction to Mary's words, Peter and Andrew have not brought the peace to which the Saviour had called them. They have simply caused suffering, as matter did by allowing a contrary nature to enter it (8.1–4).

So the Gospel of Mary shows that it is not 'the nations' who will not spare the disciples (9.5–12), but the Powers. Or, as the Letter to the Ephesians puts it:

> For we are not contending against flesh and blood, but against principalities, against the powers, against the world rulers of

this present darkness, against the spiritual hosts of wickedness in the heavenly places (Ephesians 6.12).

The proclamation of the gospel does not provoke the danger; the danger is already there. The danger arises with the fall of matter. The gospel is clearly a weapon for combating the Powers and emerging as victor from the combat.

Here we have arrived at the message of the Gospel of Mary. The call which the Gospel makes to the reader is simple: 'Proclaim the gospel!' Or, as the Saviour himself says:

Go then and preach the gospel of the kingdom (EvMar 8.22).

However, the disciples fear the danger that the proclamation of 'the gospel of the kingdom of the Human One' will bring with it (9.6–12). Mary then tells them about the protective grace of the Human One. After the intermezzo with Andrew and Peter, it is Levi who picks up the thread again:

Let us preach the gospel (EvMar 18.18).

And indeed, at the end of the Gospel of Mary the disciples set out single-mindedly (19.1–2).

The question is what 'the gospel of the kingdom of the Human One' means. In the Gospel of Mary as discovered the word kingdom is not given any further content. However, the expression 'the Human One' is. It is said of him:

For the Human One is within you.
Follow after him. Those who seek him will find him (EvMar 8.18–21).

These words are most reminiscent of the Gospel of John. There Jesus is portrayed as the Human One who has to be glorified (cf. John 12.23; 17.5). The Human One is the one who has come from heaven and who will return to heaven after he has done his work on earth. At the same time another movement is mentioned. As well as the movement from above downwards and back upwards again, there is a movement from outside inwards. Jesus will no longer be with his disciples in an earthly form, but in a spiritual way. In a prayer to God shortly before his arrest he puts it like this:

Father, I desire that they also, whom you have given me, may be where I am, to behold your glory which you have given me in your love for me before the foundation of the world. O righteous Father, the world has not known you, but I have known you; and these know that you have sent me. I made known to them your name, and I will make it known, that the love with which you have loved me may be in them, and I in them (John 17.24–26).

With the departure of the Human One (the movement upwards), at the same time the movement inwards is realized. The earthly figure of the Human One is also already no longer there: the disciples take him with them in their innermost depths. So they can look on the glory which God has given them. They can ask for his counsel; he continues to make the name of God known. And they can continue to experience the love which goes out from God and which is revealed in the Human One.

In the Gospel of Mary, too, the Human One is the same as the Saviour (9.5–12). Moreover the Gospel calls him 'the Blessed One' (8.12) and 'the Good' (7.17; cf. 8.18; 9.20–23).
The Saviour says of the Good:

That is why the Good came into your midst, to those who belong to all Nature, in order to restore it to its root (EvMar 7.17–20).

The basis of this is the notion which is worked out on pp.7 and 8 of the Gospel, that matter consists of an almost inextricable tangle of Nature, formations and creations. They are each to be dissolved down to their own roots. Nature will detach itself from matter and fix itself to what is its sole nature. Then everything will come out well.

For because matter has involved itself with an opposite nature, suffering comes into being: suffering which need not have been from the beginning. Since then there has been confusion.

The disciples must not become involved in what is not part of Nature. Nor must they allow themselves to be dominated by rules which the Saviour himself has not given. If they avoid these things they will no longer fall victim as matter to suffering and confusion, but produce the peace which belongs to the Human One.

People can go along with the adultery that matter has committed with an opposite nature. That is sin. They can also be true to the root of their existence: as matter they belong to Nature.

It is not easy to make out what the term 'Nature' could mean on particular occasions, simply from pp. 7 and 8, without knowing what was on the previous pages. The word can be quite neutral and denote the make-up of something, its essence, its origin or form, or its growth; but it is also possible that there is a more evocative reference to the divine principle which holds the cosmos together.

A philosophical tendency which was very influential in the first and second centuries, the Stoa, saw Nature as the divine primal ground of the world. According to the Stoa, the restless multiplicity of what exists has its meaningful unity in Nature. A famous quotation from the second-century emperor Marcus Aurelius runs:

O Nature, from you is all, in you is all, to you all is related (*Meditations* IV 23).

The Stoa called on men to live in accord with Nature and not to allow themselves to be distracted by the fate which befalls human beings and by the rules and laws that there are. The important thing is to achieve inner order, which embraces a confusing multitude of longings and ideas.

The lack of Nature in human beings is expressed in the suffering of the soul. This suffering is contrary to Nature. Nature is present in human beings as understanding, as thought (*logos*). Thought leads to four main virtues: understanding, braveness, self-control and justice.

According to Max Pohlenz, an expert on the Stoa, Stoic knowledge was part of the general development in the first and second century.[21] At every level of the population the most important thought and terminology was deeply influenced by the Stoa. That came about through popular orators who, all over the Hellenistic world, called on people to achieve inner perfection and a high moral standard in the midst of the many changes.

It is not inconceivable that the Gospel of Mary has used the framework of Stoic thought to make clear to a predominantly non-Jewish circle of readers who the Human One is and what he stands for.

In Stoic thought it is free will which makes a person decide for a life in accordance with Nature. The Gospel of Mary begins from the idea that more is needed here. The cosmos is not as harmonious as the Stoa thinks. Matter has not kept to Nature, but has surrendered itself to something contrary to Nature. That is the origin of the 'confusion in the whole body' (8.5–6), the 'whole body' which is an image of the cosmos.

So the Human One is needed to restore matter to Nature and thus to combat suffering and confusion.

In the Stoa the highest attainable ideal is that of the wise, the perfect man. The wise man can control his emotions to such a degree that one can speak of *apatheia*. That is a high degree of tranquillity which arises from the fact that life in all its facets is guided by the good divine Providence. This Providence has ordered all things for the best and also gives men the power to overcome heaviness. Thought can learn to control the emotions, making the way really free for a virtuous life. In the Gospel of Mary it is not the control of the emotions which is contrasted with the suffering and confusion of the cosmos, but the peace of the Human One. It is not a person's own capacity for thought which brings redemption, but the Human One. The disciples can bring forth his peace. If they seek the Human One within them, they will find him. They must follow him, proclaim the gospel of the kingdom of the Human One, and not make any laws other than what he has made.

In the Stoa the divine law of Nature is contrasted with the laws made by human beings. The Gospel of Mary opposes the one law of the Human One to other laws and rules. We do not know from the Gospel as found what is the content of the one law which the Saviour has made. One can clearly think of the one commandment which according to all the New Testament witnesses Jesus has given, and which the Gospel of John puts like this:

A new commandment I give to you, that you love one another; even as I have loved you, that you also love one another. By this it will be known that you are my disciples, if you have love for one another (John 13.34–35).

This is the commandment which Paul calls the fulfilling of the Law of Moses and a way which leads much further upwards than the highest gifts (Rom.13.8–10; I Cor.12.31–13.13).

It is important to look for redemption, liberation, in reality from the Human One and not to make any other rules or laws than the one that he has made (9.1–4; 18.18–21). According to the Gospel, making laws and rules as the lawgiver does brings with it the danger that the disciples will get imprisoned by them. The question is who is meant by the 'lawgiver' here. This is the only place in the Gospel of Mary as we have it which could indicate a specifically Gnostic context. In that case the lawgiver could be the demiurge, the god of the creation who wants to imprison human beings in the creation. However, the Greek word used for 'lawgiver' is quite a general term. For example, 'the lawgiver' can be the civil government of a city or a state. In Jewish thought the word in fact applies to God, but it can also refer to Moses and even to the rabbis. That is also the case in Christian terminology. The lawgiver stands for God or for Christ but also for the church government. And as for being held prisoner by the law, this is an idea which, for example, someone like Paul knows, without needing to assume that there is a true God who is not the god of the creation (see Rom.7.6).

In the Gospel of Mary, Peter and Andrew do not heed the Saviour's warning against rules and laws which are other than the one that he himself has made. They add an extra law, even two:

1. In their view the brothers need not listen to a woman.

2. In their view only the knowledge and interpretation of the brothers should determine the truth-content of what others add about their contact with the Redeemer.

The Gospel of Mary resolutely rejects both claims.

Views of Mary

In this section we shall be looking at the different views of Mary Magdalene which the Gospel of Mary offers us. Peter and Andrew have their own ideas here. Levi reacts to them. Mary speaks about herself. And it is very important to note that the author of the Gospel of Mary also has a say.

Peter, Andrew and Levi on Mary

Three of the brothers talk about Mary: Peter, Andrew and Levi. They do not occur as a threesome in the New Testament Gospels. There we find Peter, James and John. The Gospel of Peter does refer to them. After the crucifixion, when the disciples go each to his home, full of sorrow, Peter relates:

> But I, Simon Peter, and my brother Andrew took our nets and went to the sea. And there was with us Levi, the son of Alphaeus, whom the Lord had called away from the custom-house (Gospel of Peter 14).

That is the end of the part of the Gospel of Peter that has been discovered. It is a great shame that the fragment ends here. Originally this part would certainly have been followed by an appearance of the risen Christ and a conversation with him. It would have been fascinating to compare this with what we find in the Gospel of Mary.

It is not clear whether 'the brothers' in the Gospel of Mary means only Peter, Andrew and Levi. Perhaps there were more brothers; and perhaps there were also more sisters than Mary Magdalene.

At all events, of the brothers only Peter, Andrew and Levi speak. Peter says:

> Sister, we know that the Saviour loved you more than the rest of the women. Tell us the words of the Saviour which you remember, the things that you know and we do not, nor have we heard them (EvMar 10.1–6).

We can make out from the initial 'sister' that Peter sees Mary as a fellow-believer. They are brother and sister, both children of the one Father.

It also emerges that she occupies a special position: the Saviour loved her more than the other women. That is striking. Although Peter accepts Mary as a fellow-believer, he compares the Redeemer's love for her not with that for the other believers, but with that for the other women. For Peter, Mary is a fellow-believer, but in addition above all also a woman. It is precisely this attitude which hampers him later in the Gospel.

It is not very clear what Peter means by 'love more'. It seems to be a spiritual love, because he connects it directly with 'know'. At all events the remark about 'loving more' leads Peter to ask Mary 'what you know and we do not'.

There is also a similar connection between knowing and loving in the Gospel of John. There Jesus says to his disciples:

> No longer do I call you servants, for the servant does not know what his master is doing; but I have called you friends, for all that I have heard from my Father I have made known to you (John 15.15).

Knowing more means having a more intense contact.

For Peter, Mary is a fellow-believer and a woman. She is special because the Saviour has made known to her more of his teaching than he did to the brothers. She can supplement the knowledge of the brothers. That Peter finds that difficult to swallow emerges from his indulgent comment that the Saviour loved her more than the other women.

Andrew has a clearer view of Mary. When she has spoken, he turns to the brothers with the question:

> 'Tell me, what do you (wish to) say about the things that she has spoken?
> I at least do not believe that the Saviour said these things. For these teachings seem to be strange ideas' (EvMar 17.11–15).

Andrew does not believe that Mary is really telling what she has heard from the Saviour. It is not clear whether he thinks that she is lying, or fantasizing, or wants to make herself seem important, or whatever. It is certainly clear that like Peter he does not find it necessary to discuss the substance with her. He too turns to the brothers.

As I remarked earlier, in contrast to Andrew and to some degree also to Peter, Levi takes Mary's contribution quite seriously. He applies her words by comparing Peter with 'these adversaries'. He says:

Peter, you have always been hot-tempered. Now I see you arguing with the woman like these adversaries. If the Saviour made her worthy, who are you indeed to reject her? Surely the Saviour knows her very well. That is why he loved her more than us (EvMar 18.7-15).

According to Levi, the Saviour has made Mary worthy. Unlike Peter he can say, 'He loved her more than us'. The reason he gives is: 'Surely the Saviour knows her very well. That is why he loved her more than us.'

So Levi goes further than Peter in his estimation of Mary than Peter. Peter cannot explain the Saviour's preference for Mary. He tries to accept this as a fact while suggesting female attraction as a cause. Like Peter, Levi too makes a connection between loving and knowing (10.1-6), but Levi can accept the fact that the Saviour revealed more to Mary and that he had more intense contact with her than with the brothers. He has no difficulty in accepting her words, because he begins from the fact that the Saviour has chosen her himself to fulfil this role.

Mary on herself

Mary does not say anything about herself in the Gospel of Mary. But we can discover something about her, at least about the view of Mary which the author of the Gospel wants to give us.

When Peter asks Mary to relate what she knows and the brothers do not, she says without hesitation:

What is hidden from you I shall tell to you (EvMar 10.8).

She is evidently familiar with the idea that she indeed remembers things about the Saviour which the others do not know about. It is natural for her to share these memories.

Then she relates that she saw the Lord in a vision and later entered into a conversation with him. In it the Saviour said:

Blessed are you, because you are not shaken when you see me (EvMar 10.14-15).

As Mary remembers it, the Saviour described her as 'not being shaken' when she saw him in a vision. And he calls her blessed for that. Mary clearly did not find it a surprising experience to see the Lord apart from his earthly presence. She wants to know more.

The next time we hear anything about Mary's view of herself is when Andrew and Peter have cast doubt on the trustworthiness of her words. Weeping, she says to them:

> My brother Peter, what are you thinking? Do you suppose that I devised this, alone, in my heart, or that I am deceiving the Saviour? (EvMar 18.2–5).

Mary is convinced that she has handed on the words of the Saviour faithfully. The message is clear: 'Peter, of course I am telling the truth, for if I were inventing something about the Saviour I would be deceiving not only the brothers but also the Saviour.'

The author on Mary

The author of the Gospel of Mary speaks implicitly through all the figures who say anything in the Gospel. However, he (or she) also explicitly plays a part in the person of the narrator. The narrator speaks seven times, four times with reference to Mary. Twice the remarks are about outward perception.

When the disciples remain behind weeping after the departure of the Human One, the author relates:

> Then Mary stood up, embraced them all, and said . . . (EvMar 9.12–13).

And almost at the end of the Gospel, after the words of Andrew and Peter, the author says:

> Then Mary wept and said . . . (18.1).

The two other times that the author speaks of Mary are observations which are partly lost to view. When Mary has spoken to the weeping disciples on p.9, the author remarks:

> When Mary said these things, she turned their hearts inwards to the Good, and they began to practise the words of the Saviour (EvMar 9.20–23).

And when Mary has spoken on p.17 the author says:

When Mary had said these things, she shut her mouth, because it was to this point that the Saviour had spoken with her (EvMar 17.7–9).

From the four times that the narrator speaks we can see that he wants to depict Mary as a woman with strong feelings and actions. She embraces the disciples (like the Saviour in 8.12–13), and encourages them when encouragement is needed. She weeps when two of her fellow-believers put her integrity in doubt and expresses the consequences of their doubt.

The author also shows that Mary has influence. She knows how to turn the hearts of the disciples inwards, so that they get to the Good. In other words, she directs the attention of the disciples inwards, to where the Human One is.

Finally, the author bears witness that Mary is reliable. She hands on the words of the Saviour as he has spoken them to her. This last feature above all shows that the author is clearly adopting a particular position. He or she is not a reporter trying to give a detached account of the discussion about Mary. The author is on Mary's side. He or she is convinced of Mary's integrity and of her importance for the Christian message. Mary remembers sayings of Jesus which the other disciples appear not to know. Moreover, according to the author she has the gift of actually helping people to seek the Human One within them.

What Mary has to say

The Gospel of Mary is the only writing in antiquity in which Mary speaks for pages and tells her story. She encourages the disciples with her faith and describes the instruction that she has been given. She talks of grace and Being, about the treasure and the way upwards.

On grace and Being

The first time that we find Mary speaking is in a tense situation soon after the Saviour's farewell and mission charge. The disciples are very sad and cannot hold back their tears. They are afraid that in preaching the gospel they will call down upon themselves the same suffering as was inflicted on him. This is a justified fear, as history has shown. The disciples ask a fundamental question, about the significance of preaching the gospel. Jesus' suffering is still before their eyes, large as life. The first readers must have been thinking here of the actual persecution of believers in their time.

Mary shakes off this anxiety. She embraces the disciples and says:

> Do not weep and do not grieve, and do not make two hearts, for his grace will be with you all and will protect you. Rather let us praise his greatness, because he has prepared us. He has made us Human Being (EvMar 9.14–23).

Mary sets praise over against sorrow and despair. In her eyes the suffering of the Lord does not have the last word, but his greatness. This is a greatness which has been shown to the disciples themselves: the Saviour has made them 'Human Being'. The fact that Mary here specifically uses the generic term for 'Man' and not the term denoting the male, as happens, for example, in the Gospel of Thomas and in the Letter to the Ephesians, does not mean that here she is presenting an androgynous image.[22] It means that Mary does not speak in terms of male and female, as was very customary in her time. Here the Gospel of Mary comes close to the original teaching of Jesus.

According to Mary, the work of the Saviour consists in the recreation of persons as Human Beings. She speaks about this with reference to the suffering that the brothers fear. Earlier the Saviour himself spoke about this work in connection with sin. There is no sin, but there are people who commit adultery. They do not hold fast to Nature, but as matter allow themselves to be dragged along by the force of attraction exercised by that which is contrary to Nature. The Good has come to restore matter to Nature. This adultery of matter and the human soul underlies sickness, death, suffering and confusion. However, the disciples are one in heart, beyond confusion, and through the Human One can bring forth his peace which is within them.

It is possible that Mary is referring back to this teaching with her words 'he has made us Human Being'. Being Human then consists in the indwelling of the Human One. Indeed, being Human is thus seen as the consequence of an act of creation, but at the same time it calls for activity. The Human One must be followed and sought (EvMar 8.15–27).

The disciples are not doing that in this moment of anxiety. What the Saviour warned against is happening to them. They are making 'two hearts', and not abiding 'without mixing' (EvMar 8.8). Their heart is torn and inwardly divided: one part is directed towards Nature, and one part towards what is contrary to Nature. Mary calls on the disciples to go by the Saviour completely. He has come especially in order to redeem those who by origin belong to Nature from that which is contrary to Nature. She reminds them of their re-creation and of his grace, and of his loving care which will protect them.

On the treasure

The second time that we find Mary speaking, she is doing so at Peter's request. Rest has returned. Mary has turned the hearts of the brothers inwards towards the Good. They are practising his words. Peter asks Mary to relate those words of the Saviour which she knows are still unknown to the others. She then gives an account of a conversation about his teaching which he had with her alone. The occasion for this was that she had seen him in a vision and had told him about it. Only part of the account of this conversation which Mary gives has been preserved. The teaching about the treasure, the *nous*, ends abruptly, and that does not make interpretation easy. The *nous* is a complicated concept in Hellenistic thought, certainly when combined with the word *pneuma*. Both can indicate the human possibility of coming into contact with the divine. Both can refer to a part of the soul that brings order. And both can also stand for the divine itself.

Furthermore, the term *nous* can have different meanings when it refers to human capacities. It means sense and understanding, but also insight and concept, thought and purpose, disposition and moral attitude.

When the Saviour praises Mary for not being shaken, he refers to the *nous* as the reason for this:

For where the *nous* is, there is the treasure (EvMar 10.15).

Thus the *nous* seems to be the faculty which makes it possible for Mary not to be shaken when she sees his vision.

The Greek word which was probably used in the original text is very evocative. Being shaken is compared to the restless tossing of the sea. The same image is used in the Letter of James for the making of two hearts. According to the letter, anyone who does this and is thus inwardly divided is like a wave driven and tossed by the wind (James 1.6–8). The word often occurs in the Greek translation of the Psalms. Here being unshaken is a feature of those who direct their lives by God. Thus the Psalmist says:

> I keep the Lord always before me; because he is at my right hand, I shall not be shaken (Psalm 16.8).[23]

The *nous* is the treasure, the 'treasure in earthen vessels' (II Cor.4.5–7). Could the *nous* be the organ which can 'keep the Lord always before me'? The next passage seems to suggest this.

When Mary asks whether one sees the vision with the spirit or with the soul, he replies:

> He does not see it with the soul or with the spirit, but with the *nous* which is between the two (EvMar 10.20–22).

So we come to know more about the *nous*. The *nous* is not only the organ which keeps Mary from being shaken. It is also the organ which sees the vision, something that the spirit and the soul do not know. Moreover the place of the *nous* is disclosed to us: between the spirit and the soul.

First of all we must seek to understand Mary's question.

Mary thinks in the categories of soul and spirit. In the Stoa the soul is the seat of perception by the senses. The spirit is the principle that holds the cosmos together, that gives the body life as breath, and that orders the turbulence of the soul. The human spirit is in direct contact with the divine Spirit, and at the same time also with everything that makes an impact on the soul. Thus Mary with her two categories should really presuppose three: the soul, the spirit and the Spirit, the last two of which have the same nature.

There were two views about dreams at that time. One said that the spirit rested, the senses of the soul took over and produced ghostly images. The other said that the spirit parted from the soul and now, detached from the confusing impressions of the soul, could converse freely with the spiritual and even see the Godhead.[24] Perhaps on the basis of this we may suppose that Mary's question about precisely what sees the vision is the question: revelation or projection? She asks whether the vision comes from the divine Spirit or from her own soul.

The Saviour introduces a new category in answering Mary's question about soul and spirit: the place of the *nous* is between the soul and the spirit. Now we no longer have 'soul, spirit, Spirit', but 'soul, *nous*, Spirit'. He exchanges the human spirit for the *nous*, which can also happen in the Stoa, but he leaves the Spirit, instead of exchanging the Spirit for *nous*. In so doing he creates an opposition. The *nous* as a human category is now separate from the spirit, which has thus become a transcendent instead of an immanent divine category.

Is it possible that here the Saviour is presenting in a way comprehensible to Hellenistic ears the Jewish view that God is transcendent and nevertheless can be known by human beings, at least partially? Also through a vision?

If we look at Philo, who set himself the task of explaining the faith of Israel to a Hellenistic audience, we find the same categories, and it also becomes clearer what it could mean that the *nous* has its place between the soul and the spirit. In his exegesis of the creation story, Philo begins from the fact that God blows the spirit into the *nous*. Every living human being breathes, but the true breath of life is to be found in the *nous*.[25] The *nous* which has the spirit blown into it has the task of guiding the soul. Simply by virtue of that the human being changes from a dull and blind soul into a spiritual and truly living being. Philo calls this *nous* the real Human Being in man. This expression makes us think of Mary's words 'he has made us Human Being'. He also calls the *nous* 'father', 'teacher', 'pilot of the soul', 'cause of all good' and 'shepherd of the powers of our soul'. The *nous* is related to the body as a 'god'.[26]

It is difficult to find anything like a 'doctrine' in the Gospel of Mary as we have it. But we can say on the basis of what we have now discovered in Philo that we are on the track of a certain kind of argument. The Saviour, the Good, has come to recreate the human being who was once created. There was confusion and suffering in the cosmos because matter had allowed in a 'contrary nature'. Redemption consists in the fact that the Saviour again blows the spirit into the *nous*, the mind, which has the task of ordering the turbulence of the soul and seeking God. It makes its entry into human beings. They thus gain power to escape the adultery with what is contrary to Nature.

On the way upwards

From the conversation about the mind, about the *nous*, we abruptly move to the fate of the soul. The Saviour tells of its struggle. The closer it gets to heaven, the more powerful the opposition becomes. Whereas at first individual powers want to restrain it, the last power is sevenfold.

Given the structure of the Gospel, we can assume that the account of the soul is the answer to a question of Mary's. However, the question is on one of the missing pages. That means that we have to guess at the context in which the Saviour relates these things about the soul. It seems reasonable to assume that Mary has asked about the new category which the Saviour has given her and which he has placed between the soul and the spirit. The missing part of the work would then be about the *nous* and the spirit, while the part that has been preserved is about the soul and the *nous*. Granted, the word *nous* does not appear after p.15, but the answers that the soul gives to the powers bear witness to the knowledge which the mind can have through divine revelation.

We saw earlier that in Hellenistic thought, and above all in the Stoa, the soul is the seat of the senses. Through the senses it receives confusing impressions.

Its task is to order the turbulence of the soul so that there is room for moral action. Philo writes an account of this in connection with the story of the flood:

It is proper to note also that when confusion comes upon the mind, and, like a flood, in the life of the world mounds of affairs are erected at one time, it is impossible to sow or conceive or give birth to anything good. But when discords and attacks and the gradual invasions of monstrous thought are kept off, then being dried, like the fertile and productive places of the earth, it produces virtues and excellent things (*Questions and Answers on Genesis* II, 49).

Besides this emphasis on personal responsibility, the Hellenistic view of life is steeped in the thought that life is in the hands of fate, Greek *heimarmene*, which means something like 'the series of causes'. The Stoa had convinced people of the inescapable regularity by which all things run their course. The soul is determined by the body and by the natural surroundings in which it is born. At the same time it is influenced by the heavenly bodies. From the planets it has received its capacity for ordering, its sensuality, and the growth which is necessary for the body: the seven parts of the soul which were already mentioned in Chapter 2. The whole cosmos and thus, in the materialistic-holistic view of the Stoa, also the human being, basically consist of the four elements of earth, water, air and fire. The ethereal fire is the prime element which permeates all things and holds them together. That is nature, the spirit. In the human being the divine fire is mixed with air: the breath of life. The seven planets stand closest to the fire. The earth is furthest away from it.[27]

In the light of this Hellenistic thought it is striking that in Mary's account the Saviour uses the figures four and seven and arranges them in such a way that the fourth power, which is closest to heaven, has seven forms. The spiritual forces which, according to the Saviour, lay siege to the soul thus seem to be analogous to the material powers which for the Stoa make the soul and the cosmos what they are. It is not easy to draw conclusions here without knowing the course of the conversation between Mary and the Saviour on pp.11–14.

However, we can refer back to the conversation between the Saviour and the disciples contained on pp.7–8.

It then seems evident that in the conversation with Mary on pp.15–17 the Saviour is defining what is 'contrary to Nature' more closely, as the powers of Darkness, Desire, Ignorance and Wrath. The soul has allied itself with them as it has with the elements of earth, water, air and fire to itself. Redemption consists of being loosed from these: heaven and earth will be released. What belongs to Nature will be restored in its roots. The

soul can effectively combat the powers by pointing out to them –
and also to itself – their ultimate powerlessness. All in all, they
appear not to have any power over the soul, and that is made clear
to the reader in an ironical way.

Desire betrays its blindness in its claim to power. It did not see
the soul when she was on the way to earth, in contrast to the soul,
who certainly seems to see Desire very well and remains apart
from it, like clothing from the body. Ignorance betrays her lack of
knowledge. The soul knows that wickedness has her in its grasp,
as Ignorance states. However, she notes why that is: since she has
not held on to wickedness, wickedness grasped her. Wrath points
to the soul as a killer of human beings and as someone who makes
these places powerless. The suggestion is the same as that in
connection with Desire and Ignorance: the soul must not think
that she comes from heaven and is going back there. Wrath, too,
displays itself. Indeed the soul leaves places behind powerless. But
these are not the places which Wrath means, the bodies. The soul
has herself made Wrath powerless: its first three forms have been
overcome. Thanks to the heavenly liberation and its own struggle
the soul can now receive the Rest in silence.

In general, it is assumed that this description of the fate of the
soul describes a 'journey of the soul' after death. People were
convinced that after death the soul would go back to its origin.
There are a whole series of descriptions of this journey, which is
also depicted as a struggle.[28] However, there are other writings
which describe a struggle of the soul in the present.[29]

From what we are told by the Gospel of Mary, it is difficult to
decide whether the soul's struggle is a struggle in the present or a
struggle after death. The beginning of the description of the way
of the soul is on the missing pages. But we do know the final goal,
the Rest in silence, at the time of the decisive moment of the aeon.
It seems reasonable to suppose that the decisive moment is the
moment of the 'dissolution of the All', a moment that lies in the
future. That might possibly suggest a journey after death.
However, in the case of a journey of the soul after death it is usual
to speak of seven powers, or three, or numberless powers. There
is no case of the number of powers being the same as that of
matter, namely four.[30] Perhaps we should not want to press the
Gospel into this framework of thought. It is clear that the soul

now already has to fight against Darkness, Desire, Ignorance and Wrath. And the presupposition that the victory is in prospect and has to do with a future action 'on the part of heaven' seems very likely. Whether according to the Gospel of Mary the struggle also goes on after death is something that only the missing pages could tell us.

Conclusion

At the end of the previous chapter I asked whether Mary Magdalene might perhaps have had followers. I also asked what could be the reason for the high esteem given in Gnosticism to Mary Magdalene in particular. We also wanted to know more about Peter's hostility. In this section we shall see how much further the Gospel of Mary helps us to progress here.

Mary Magdalene and her Gospel

What is the significance of Mary Magdalene having a Gospel to her name? It does not mean that she is its author. In all probability she was already dead when the Gospel was composed. Nor does the author make any effort to make us believe that Mary Magdalene herself wrote the Gospel. The title does not refer to the author, but to the content of the Gospel. At its centre stands the teaching of the Saviour as it has been understood by Mary. The author is very clear about that. Mary's behaviour and her explanation of the gospel actually proves to help people. She remembers words of Jesus which are unknown to the other first disciples. Thus those who pay no attention to her are missing part of the teaching of Jesus and leaving an important source of information untapped. Not all that long ago it was generally presupposed that everything that has to be dated later than the New Testament Gospels is based on them and made use of them. That meant that any later writing reshaped biblical events or elaborated them fantastically. The reason given for this proced-ure was that the author was satisfying curiosity or proving that he was right. In the case of the Gospel of Mary that would mean that the author was concerned to convince the readers of the truth of a particular doctrine by putting it in the mouth of Mary

Magdalene. In other words, the Gospel of Mary would say nothing about Mary Magdalene and everything about the author. The starting point of such a presupposition is that all reliable oral and written tradition about Jesus is contained in the four Gospels and stopped abruptly after that. This starting point might perhaps have been convincing in terms of dogma, but it has to be rejected historically. It is much more likely that, like the four Gospels, other writings drew on the broad stream of oral and written tradition around Jesus. Moreover, nowadays scholars no longer assume that only the authors of the four Gospels are reliable and the others by definition not.[31]

It is possible that the author of the Gospel of Mary is putting a particular doctrine into Mary Magdalene's mouth. However, we cannot assume that as a presupposition. It has to be demonstrated.

I begin with the other possibility: that the author had heard of Mary Magdalene or had known her personally and had learned to see her and her testimony as an important source of inspiration. To sound out this possibility we must return to what we discovered about Mary Magdalene in Chapter 2. She grew up in a town where both Judaism and Hellenism were known from the inside and where different nationalities came into contact with one another at the market. This town left its mark on her. She was named after it by the small group of Jesus' permanent followers – to which, as we have seen, she belonged. It is no great step from this to assume that she could have spoken alone with Jesus about questions with a more Hellenistic colouring, which she had and the others did not. This fits with Peter's assumption in the Gospel of Mary that Mary knows things which are different from the others. And it also fits the Hellenistic background that we assume behind the Gospel as a whole. The picture of Mary which the Gospel of Mary sketches out thus does not seem strange in view of what we got to know about her earlier.

Gnosis and Mary Magdalene

The other possibility is that the author wants to convince readers of a particular doctrine by putting it in the mouth of Mary Magdalene. Why Mary Magdalene in particular? If the author needed a disciple to make his teaching carry conviction, any male disciple whatsoever would have been a better choice than Mary Magdalene, given the Jewish and Roman view of women. Perhaps the author wanted to put Mary, the witness to the resurrection, to the fore as an esoteric figure. Perhaps the author needed a woman to give voice to the discussion about being a woman.[32]

The other question which we must raise is whether the Gospel of Mary in fact contains a particular doctrine, the legitimacy of which the author wants to defend with reference to the first disciples. It is impossible to give a satisfactory answer to this question. Too much of the Gospel of Mary is missing. We can certainly say that we have found no particular doctrine. The Gospel of Mary as we now know it explains to a predominantly non-Jewish readership the brokenness of creation, the fall, and the liberation from the fall by the Saviour. Here use is made of Hellenistic terminology. This is not structural, so that it seems to be based on a particular doctrine, but rather creative, parallel to the way in which Philo makes use of Hellenistic thought. Thus the Gospel of Mary seems to be an attempt to translate into Hellenistic terminology the teaching of Jesus and what happened to and through him; the Gospel is not advocating a particular doctrine.

However, it is striking that the Gospel of Mary was preserved in the fifth century along with three other writings, of which at least one is clearly Gnostic. It is also striking that at the beginning of the third century Mary Magdalene is associated by Hippolytus with the Gnostic teaching of the Naassenes and that the Pistis Sophia, which is clearly Gnostic, assigns her an equally major role in the same century. Does that then mean that we must assume that Gnostic doctrine (in its classical sense) underlies the Gospel of Mary and that it is in fact the intention of the author to put Gnostic arguments into the mouth of Mary Magdalene? I don't think so. In the Gospel of Mary we see the germ of what later becomes the important place that Mary Magdalene gets in Gnosticism.[33] Just as the letters of Paul could be interpreted in Gnostic terms, so too was the teaching of Mary Magdalene. Mary's recollections of the Saviour are different, as Andrew rightly remarks in the Gospel of Mary. But this is not because they presuppose another teaching. They presuppose a Hellenistic background.

Peter and Mary Magdalene

The hostility of Peter to Mary Magdalene is often interpreted symbolically. In that case Peter stands for the orthodoxy of the early church and Mary Magdalene for Gnosticism. On this interpretation, in the Gospel of Mary the opponents named by Levi are the orthodox Christians. In both philosophical and religious debates it was usual to claim that opponents could only persuade women. Thus Peter is employing the usual polemic in attacking Mary because she is a woman. Levi takes this up in order to accuse Peter of choosing a woman as his target instead of dealing with the real adversaries.[34]

I cannot go along with this interpretation. We have seen that the adversaries whom Levi mentions are the powers. Moreover, Levi is not asserting that Peter is one of the adversaries, but that he is like them. Nor did we see Mary as a typical representative of Gnosticism, and there is no question of rhetorical polemic. Peter does not bring up Mary because she has been so readily influenced by Gnostic ideas, He defends the view that men need not listen to a woman.

This fits in with the ambivalence over women disciples that we already found in the New Testament Gospels. It also fits in with the fact that women were not accepted as witnesses in the Jewish tradition, and that Roman legislation regarded them as weak, insignificant, frivolous and fickle.[35] Indeed Peter represents an orthodox view. However, this is not one that is specifically associated with Gnosticism. He represents an orthodox view about women who have something to say.

To sum up: we conclude that the Gospel of Mary does not just tell us something about its author and what he has to say, but that the Gospel is also really about Mary Magdalene. That means that Mary Magdalene had followers who saw her and her teaching as an important source of inspiration. It was probably her partially Hellenistic background which was the underlying cause of the intense relationship with Jesus which the Gospel relates. She knows more things than the others, not because she is a special initiate but because her background is different. This also explains the hostility of Peter (or his followers). Peter came from an ordinary Jewish village, Mary Magdalene came from a town which was a Jewish–Hellenistic centre of trade.[36] That means that in all probability Peter was hardly familiar with women who like Mary were used to a certain freedom of movement.

The gospel of Mary Magdalene is a Hellenistic rendering of what meant most to her in the teaching and the figure of Jesus. The Gospel of Mary is an account of this. It gives a central place to the question of suffering: suffering in general and the suffering of the Human One in particular. Mary contrasts this with his greatness. The Human One has shown the deeper cause of suffering and has enabled his followers finally to overcome it.

Peace and rest are possible, and it is the task of the disciples to bring this about.

5

Mary Magdalene

Then Mary stood up . . . and said, 'Do not weep and do not grieve and do not make two hearts, for his grace will be with you all and will protect you. Rather let us praise his greatness, because he has prepared us. He has made us Human Being' (Gospel of Mary 9.12–20).

I began this book on the presupposition that it must be worth while setting out systematically what the earliest traditions can tell us about Mary Magdalene. My presupposition was that they could tell us a good deal. Mary Magdalene was a follower of Jesus from the first. She was one of the few to be at the crucifixion and burial. She was the first to proclaim the resurrection.

We left on one side the image which made Mary Magdalene popular down the centuries. We saw that the attractive, sinful woman, the sister of Martha and Lazarus who repented and did penance, was no more than a picture. We went in search of who Mary Magdalene could have been, in search of her story.

What has our quest yielded?

The quest at an end

First of all we have above all found new images. The New Testament Gospels, the various church fathers, the two church orders, the Acts of Philip, the Gospel literature outside the Bible – every text gives its own impression of Mary Magdalene. But in contrast to the mediaeval picture, behind these images from antiquity we have been able to assume a historical nucleus. We have tried to trace it.

Mary Magdalene: disciple and apostle

We have seen that Mary Magdalene was one of the small circle of

Jesus' permanent followers. She was a disciple like the twelve disciples. Jesus was her teacher and she was his pupil, from the bright beginning to the bitter end.

We do not know why she became a disciple. We have inferred Mary's background from her surname, Magdalene. Through the recent excavations in Mejdel, through the writings of Flavius Josephus and other written evidence from antiquity we formed a picture of the town of Magdala. From that we inferred that Mary Magdalene grew up a Jew in a town on which Hellenistic culture had left its mark and that she must have been familiar with people of different nationalities and cultures. She was a witness to the great differences between rich and poor, to the terrors of the Roman occupation and opposition to it, and all this in an environment in which nature showed its best side: fish in abundance, water in abundance, a wide range of fertile trees and shrubs. We set this background alongside the teaching and person of Jesus. That led us to reconstruct what must have moved Mary Magdalene to become a disciple of Jesus. She was under the impact of the non-violent, spiritual and healing character of the kingdom of God as personified in Jesus. She was struck by his conviction that God has mercy on all without distinction, and by his attention to people's dispositions. The Gospel of Luke is the only writing which tells us something more of Mary's choice of discipleship; according to Luke, contact with Jesus was an enormous liberation for her.

We concluded that Mary Magdalene was a courageous and persistent disciple, as is witnessed by the fact that she seems to have been one of the few at the crucifixion and the burial and that she also went to look at the tomb later. The witnesses to this event differ. There is a central insight that the Lord is risen. However, each New Testament Gospel gives it its own content to Mary Magdalene's function and has its own version of it. Here two themes are to be distinguished, the precise content of Mary's message and her role towards the other disciples.

According to Mark, Matthew and Luke, at the resurrection this role is concerned with words of revelation which were already known to the disciples as a group before Jesus' death. In John it involves a new testimony which Mary Magdalene herself hears from the risen Christ.

ZZ1300

John depicts Mary Magdalene as a disciple and apostle. Matthew limits her apostolate to the eleven disciples. Luke makes it clear that she has the apostolate on her own authority and as a result causes confusion. Mark addresses his readers with a call to be apostles, both men and women.

We have concluded from the Gospel of Mary that Mary Magdalene must have had followers who experienced her and her formulation of the gospel as an inspiration. She thus proclaimed the gospel, and in so doing was an apostle in the general sense of the word as Mark and John understand it. Where her apostolate took her, we do not know. The origin of the Gospel of Mary could give us more information, but that is not clear. We found another indication in Paul's letter to the Romans, where a Mary seems to have been known to the community in Rome, but that was not convincing. The other indications are relatively late. The Acts of Philip were written in Asia Minor in the fourth century, the Pistis Sophia probably in the third century in Egypt. Both options return later. The seventh-century patriarch of Jerusalem, Modestus, relates that Mary Magdalene preached the Gospel from Ephesus and also suffered martyrdom there.[1] A life of Mary Magdalene probably written by Pseudo-Cyril of Jerusalem in the fifth century reports that she remained in Jerusalem for a long time. She was there after the death of Mary the mother of Jesus, by whom she was set over the apostles. The apostles proclaimed the gospel from Jerusalem, whereas Mary Magdalene received secret revelations from Christ. From Jerusalem she later went to Egypt.[2]

Mary Magdalene: *woman*

The fact that Mary Magdalene was a woman played a role in our quest in all kinds of ways. It already began with the earliest sources. We noted that above all the first three New Testament Gospels proved ambivalent over the women disciples. They have to be mentioned as witnesses, but the way in which they are introduced is abrupt and restrained. We compared that with the not particularly positive Roman and Jewish view of women as witnesses. We also saw that the fact that there were women disciples cannot have been regarded warmly. Both Jewish tradition and Roman legislation propagated motherhood as the only worthy content of a woman's life. Nor do the Gospels anywhere call Mary Magdalene and the other women real disciples, unless they are included when the masculine plural of the word 'disciples' is used. However, in the church fathers and the Gospel literature outside the Bible the female form of the word 'disciple' does appear.

The fact that Mary Magdalene was a woman made it possible for the church fathers to portray her as a counterpart of Eve, the woman who brought sin into the world. For the church fathers Mary Magdalene is the 'new Eve'; she may bring the message of redemption. So she seems to be almost in a line with Christ, who is seen as the new Adam. However, nothing is less true. From Origen to Augustine the great distance between the two is emphasized.

The church orders and also, it seems, the Acts of Philip are careful that the special position of Mary Magdalene does not prompt women believers to take too great freedoms.[3]

The First Apocalpyse of James allows us to hear another voice: all women are called to show their joy over the women disciples. Through them it has proved that the powerless vessels which women are can become strong through the insight that is in them through Christ.

In some writings Peter is the personification of the orthodox view of women. Mary Magdalene is afraid of him 'because he hates our sex', and he is afraid of Mary: he is anxious that this 'new Eve' should not become influential. 'Let Mary depart from us,' he says, 'since women are not worthy of Life', and he asks the brothers, 'Are we to turn about and all listen to her? Has he chosen her above us?'

We can ask how far the fact that Mary Magdalene was a woman also consciously played a role for herself. Did she attach herself to Jesus among other things because of the open way in which he dealt with women? I have found no texts which might confirm the conjecture. Moreover according to the Dialogue of the Saviour she is unprotestingly a conversation partner in the doctrinal discussion about the 'works of femininity' which must be destroyed. She does not react when Matthew cites as words of the Lord, 'Pray where there is no woman.'[4] The other question which keeps occupying people down the centuries is whether Mary Magdalene felt attracted as a woman to Jesus. We have not come across any texts which indicate this. The texts show that she was impressed by Jesus' teaching.

Once again, beyond the myth

We began our quest with the current Western view of Mary Magdalene as penitent. We wanted to get back in time behind that picture: beyond the myth. During our quest we left more current views behind us. We saw that the small group around Jesus consisted not only of the 'twelve disciples' but also of women. We also saw that 'the four Gospels' are not the only source of knowledge about Jesus, but that more writings can be drawn on. Moreover we saw that the 'church fathers' do not represent the whole of the early Christian tradition but only part of it. Here questions necessarily arise. The church tradition has limited itself to the twelve disciples, the four Gospels and the church fathers. What has it gained in so doing? And what has it lost?

Then and now

On the basis of what we have discovered in our quest for Mary Magdalene, we have to note that at all events the church tradition lost sight of Jesus' open way of dealing with women. Jesus listened to both men and women. He entered into conversations with men and women. The church tradition chose not to do this.

For a long time I thought that women really had little to say in the first centuries. Many died giving birth, and men lived longer. The quest for Mary Magdalene has produced another picture: in the first century men asked themselves whether they needed to listen to women. That means that there were women who had something to say. It also means that it was not taken for granted that they had to keep silent. The church tradition made a choice. Perhaps this choice was unavoidable at the time. The question is whether it is defensible for churches and other Christian communities to make the same choice today.

Conclusion

We have been able to give a reasonably clear answer to the first question that we asked at the beginning of the quest for Mary Magdalene, 'Who was she?'. We have to note that this has not been so possible with the second question, 'What is her story?'. The evidence is too diverse. But we have concluded that the Gospel of Mary could be an account of what Mary Magdalene had to tell. We have also seen that its theme partially coincides with what the Gospel of John – the only source which lets her say something – says of her. When Mary Magdalene speaks, in both Gospels it is about the death of Jesus, the changed relationship to the divine, and the way upwards.

From penitent to human being

In Chapter 1 we saw how attractive the image of Mary Magdalene the penitent proved. She left behind a golden thread in pictorial art and in literature, in teaching the faith, in mysticism, liturgy and also in social work. That all was not gold, and some was dross, has been demonstrated by women like Elizabeth Moltmann-Wendel and Susan Haskins. That does not mean that Mary Magdalene the penitent does not remain a fascinating figure. However, she is not Mary Magdalene. And we wanted to know who she was and what she had to tell.

Peter Ketter thought that the need to exchange Mary Magdalene the penitent for the historical Mary Magdalene was a loss for teaching the faith. However, anyone who takes the Gospel of Mary seriously encounters a Mary Magdalene who can certainly be a source of inspiration.

Mary Magdalene the penitent says:

Do not despair, you who are prone to sin, but by my example restore your relationship with God (see p.4).

The Mary Magdalene of the Gospel of Mary says:

Do not weep and do not grieve and do not make two hearts, for his grace will be with you all and will protect you. Rather let us praise his greatness, because he has prepared us. He has made us Human Being (EvMar 9.12–20).

The penitent St Mary Magdalene remains far away and to earthly sinners sets an example of perfection.

The Mary Magdalene of the Gospel of Mary comes close. Not to men and women whom she calls, but to men and women whom she sees as being confused and anxious. She does not just set an example. She does not just bear witness to her own humanity, but to the humanity of all. Christ's loving concern and his redemptive power can be found in everyone. The human mind with new life breathed into it by him can again be the real 'pilot of the soul', the 'Human Being' in people. Christ makes clear which powers are behind suffering and confusion: Darkness, Desire, Ignorance and Wrath. He proves these Powers to be powerless. Thus the way upwards can really be taken.

Select Bibliography

Bode, Edward Lynn, *The First Easter Morning. The Gospel Accounts of the Women's Visit to the Tomb of Jesus*, Analecta Biblica 45, Rome 1970

Boer, E.A.de, 'Maria van Magdala en haar Evangelie', in G.Quispel (ed.), *Gnosis. De derde component van de Europese cultuurtraditie*, Utrecht 1988

Borg, Marcus, *Jesus. A New Vision. Spirit, Culture and the Life of Discipleship*, San Francisco 1987

Bosen, W., *Galiläa als Lebensraum und Wirkungsfeld Jesu*, Freiburg im Breisgau 1985

Bovon, François, 'Le privilège Pascal de Marie Madeleine', *New Testament Studies* 30 ,1984, 50–62

Brown, Raymond E., 'Roles of Women in the Fourth Gospel', *Theological Studies* 36, 1975, 688–99

——, 'The Burial of Jesus (Mark 15:42–47)', *The Catholic Biblical Quarterly* 50, 1988, 233–45

Coquin, R.-G. and Godron, G., 'Un encomion Copte sur Marie-Madeleine attribué à Cyrille de Jérusalem', *Bulletin de l'Institut Français d'Archéologie Orientale* 90, Cairo 1990

Corbo, Vergilio, 'La città Romana di Magdala', *Studia Hierosolymitana* I, 1976, 358–78

Corley, Kathleen, ' "Noli me tangere". Mary Magdalene in the Patristic Literature' (unpublished article)

Corpus Hermeticum, with an introduction, Dutch translation and commentary by R. van den Broek and G. Quispel, Amsterdam 1991

Culianu, Ioan Petru, *Psychanodia I. A survey of the evidence concerning the ascension of the soul and its relevance*, Leiden 1983

Dalman, G., *Arbeit und Sitte in Palastina*, Gütersloh 1937

Daube, David, *The Duty of Procreation*, Edinburgh 1977

Duperray, Eve (ed.), *Marie Madeleine dans la mystique, les arts et les lettres*, Paris 1989

Fee, Gordon D., *God's Empowering Presence. The Holy Spirit in the Letters of Paul*, Peabody 1994

Finegan, Jack, *The Archeology of the New Testament. The Life of Jesus and the Beginning of the Early Church*, revised edition, Princeton 1994

Freyne, S., *Galilee from Alexander the Great to Hadrian*, Wilmington 1980

Grenfell, Bernard P., and Hunt, Arthur S., *The Oxyrhynchus Papyri*, London 1898–

Gryson, Roger, *Le ministère des femmes dans l'église ancienne*, Recherches et synthèses, section d'histoire IV, Gembloux 1972

Guillaume, Paul-Marie, 'Marie Madeleine (St.)', in *Le Dictionnaire de la Spiritualité*, Paris 1980

Haskins, Susan, *Mary Magdalen. Myth and Metaphor*, London 1993

Heine, Susanne, *Women and Early Christianity. Are the Feminist Scholars Right?*, London 1987

Helderman, Jan, *Die Anapausis im Evangelium Veritatis. Eine vergleichende Untersuchung des valentinianisch-gnostischen Heilsgutes der Ruhe im Evangelium Veritatis und in anderen Schriften der Nag Hammadi-Bibliothek*, Nag Hammadi Studies 18, Leiden 1984

Hengel, Martin, 'Maria Magdalena und die Frauen als Zeugen', in Betz, Otto, *Abraham Unser Vater. Festschrift für Otto Michel*, Leiden 1963, 243–56

Hester, J. David, 'Dramatic Inconclusion: Irony and the Narrative Rhetoric of the Ending of Mark', *Journal for the Study of the New Testament* 57, 1995, 61–86

Holzmeister, U., 'Die Magdalenenfrage in der kirchlichen Überlieferung', *Zeitschrift für Katholische Theologie* 46, 1922, 402–22, 556–84

Jonas, Hans, *The Gnostic Religion*, Boston ²1963

Jungmann. J.A., *Missarum Solemnia. Eine genetische Erklärung der Römischen Messe*, Vienna 1958

Ketter, Peter, *The Magdalene Question*, Milwaukee 1935

King, Karen L., *Images of the Feminine in Gnosticism*, Studies in Antiquity and Christianity, Philadelphia 1988

——, 'The Gospel of Mary', in Miller, R.J. (ed.), *The Complete Gospels. Annotated Scholars Version*, California 1992

Klauck, H.-J., 'Die dreifache Maria. Zur Rezeption von Joh 19.25 in EvPhil 32', in Van Seebroeck, F., et al. (ed.), *The Four Gospels 1992. Festschrift Frans Neyrinck*, III, Louvain 1992, 2343–57

Koester. H., and Robinson, J.M., *Trajectories through Early Christianity*, Philadelphia 1971

Leisegang, Hans, *Der heilige Geist. Das Wesen und Werden der mystisch-intuitive Erkenntnis in der Philosophie und Religion der Griechen*, Darmstadt 1967

Loffreda, Stanislao, 'Magdala – Tarichea', *Bibbia e Oriente* 18, 1976 (3–4), 133–5

Lührmann, D., 'Die Griechischen Fragmente des Mariae-evangeliums P.Ox 3525 und P.Ryl 463' ,*Novum Testamentum* 30, 1988, 321–38

Luttikhuizen, G.P., *Gnostische Geschriften 1: Het Evangelie naar Maria, het Evangelie naar Filippus, de Brief van Petrus aan Filipus*, Kampen 1986

Maisch, Ingrid, *Maria Magdalena zwischen Verachtung und Verehrung. Das Bild einer Frau im Spiegel der Jahrhunderte*, Freiburg 1996

Malvern, Marjorie, *Venus in Sackcloth. The Magdalen's Origins and Metamorphoses*, London 1975

Manns, Frédéric, 'Magdala dans les sources littéraires', in *Studia Hierosolymitana. In onore del P. Bellarmino Bagatti. I Studi Archeologici*, Studium Biblicum Franciscanum, Collectio Maior 22, Jerusalem 1976, 307–37

Methuen, C, 'Widows, Bishops and the Struggle for Authority in the Didascalia Apostolorum', *Journal of Ecclesiastical History* 1995, 197–213

Moltmann-Wendel, Elisabeth, *The Women around Jesus*, London and New York 1982

Mosco, Marilene (ed.), *La Maddalena tra Sacro e Profano*, Florence 1986

Müller, Ulrich B., 'Vision und Botschaft', *Zeitschrift für Theologie und Kirche* 74, 1977, 416–48

Neyrinck, F., 'Les Femmes au Tombeau: Étude de la redaction Matthéenne (Mat. XXVIII. 1–10)', *New Testament Studies* 15, 1969, 168–90

O'Collins, Gerald, 'The Fearful Silence of Three Women (Mark 16:8c)', *Gregorianum* 69, 1988, 489–503

Pagels, Elaine, *The Gnostic Gospels*. New York 1979

Parsch, Pius, *Het jaar des Heren*, Apeldoorn 1941

Parvey, Constance F., 'The Theology and Leadership of Women in the New Testament', in Ruether, Rosemary Radford (ed.), *Religion and*

Sexism. Images of Woman in the Jewish and Christian Traditions, New York 1974, 117–49

Pasquier, A., *L'Evangile selon Marie. Texte établi et présenté*, Bibliothèque Copte de Nag Hammadi, section 'textes' 10, Quebec 1983

Perkins, Pheme, *The Gnostic Dialogue. The Early Church and the Crisis of Gnosticism*, New York 1980

Pohlenz, Max, *Die Stoa. Geschichte einer geistigen Bewegung*, Göttingen 1948

Pomeroy, Sarah B., *Goddesses, Whores, Wives and Slaves. Women in Classical Antiquity*, New York 1975

Quispel, G., 'Das Hebräerevangelium im gnostischen Evangelium nach Maria', *Vigiliae Christianae* 11, 1957, 139–44

Roberts, C.H. *Catalogue of the Greek and Latin Papyri in the John Rylands Library Manchester III. Theological and Literary Texts (Nos.457–551)*, Manchester 1938

Robinson, J.M., *The Nag Hammadi Library in English*, third completely revised edition, Leiden 1988

Roukema, R., *De uitleg van Paulus' eerste brief aan de Corinthiërs in de tweede en derde eeuw*, Kampen 1996

Rudolph, Kurt, *Gnosis*, Edinburgh 1984

Ryan, R., 'The Women from Galilee and Discipleship in Luke', *Biblical Theology Bulletin* 15, 1985, 56–9

Sanders, E.P., *The Historical Figure of Jesus*, London 1993

Saxer, Victor, *Le culte de Marie Madeleine en Occident. Des origines à la fin du moyen âge*, Cahiers d'archéologie et d'histoire 3, Paris 1959

Schmidt, C., *Pistis Sophia. Ein gnostisches Originalwerk*, Leipzig 1925

Schneemelcher, W., and Wilson, R.McL., *New Testament Apocrypha 1 and 2*, Louisville and Cambridge 1991, 1992

Schneider, Carl, *Kulturgeschichte des Hellenismus*, Munich 1967

Schottroff, Luise, 'Maria Magdalena und die Frauen am Grabe Jesu', *Evangelische Theologie* 42, 1982, 3–25

Schüssler Fiorenza, Elisabeth, 'Word, Spirit and Power: Women in Early Christian Communites', in Ruether, Rosemary and Mclaughlin, Eleanor (ed), *Female Leadership in the Jewish and Christian Traditions*, New York, 1979, 29–70

——, *In Memory of Her. A Feminist Theological Reconstruction of Christian Origins*, Boston and London 1983

Schweizer, E., 'Scheidungsrecht der jüdischen Frau? Weibliche Jünger Jesu?', *Evangelische Theologie* 42, 1982, 294–300

Sickenberger, J., 'Ist die Magdalenen-Frage wirklich unlösbar?', *Biblische Zeitschrift* 17, 1926, 63–74

Starbird, Margaret, *The Woman with the Alabaster Jar. Mary Magdalen and the Holy Grail*, Santa Fé 1993

Synek, Eva M., ' "Die andere Maria." Zum Bild der Maria von Magdala in den östlichen Kirchentraditionen', *Oriens Christianus* 79, 1995, 181–96

Tardieu, Michel, *Écrits gnostiques. Codex de Berlin*, Paris 1984

——, and Dubois, J.-D., *Introduction à la littérature gnostique, 1: Collections retrouvées avant 1945*, Paris 1986

Till, W.C., *Die gnostischen Schriften des koptischen Papyrus Berolinensis 8502*, Texte und Untersuchungen zur Geschichte der altchristlichen Literatur 60, Berlin 1955 (second edition revised by H.-M. Schenke, 1972)

Warner, Marina, *Alone of all Her Sex. The Myth and the Cult of the Virgin Mary*, London 1976

Williams, M.A., *The Immovable Race. A Gnostic Designation and the Theme of Stability in Late Antiquity*, Nag Hammadi Studies 29, Leiden 1985

Wilson, R., 'The New Testament in the Gospel of Mary', *New Testament Studies* 3, 1956/1957, 236–43

Notes

1. Beyond the Myth

1. Elaine Pagels, *The Gnostic Gospels*, New York 1979.
2. Victor Saxer, *Le culte de Marie Madeleine en Occident. Des origines à la fin du moyen âge*, Cahiers d'archéologie et d'histoire 3, Paris 1959; Marjorie Malvern, *Venus in Sackcloth. The Magdalen's Origins and Metamorphoses*, London 1975; Susan Haskins, *Mary Magdalen. Myth and Metaphor*, London 1993; and recently Ingrid Maisch, *Maria Magdalena zwischen Verachtung und Verehrung. Das Bild einer Frau im Spiegel der Jahrhunderte*, Freiburg 1996.
3. See also E.A.de Boer, 'Maria van Magdala en haar Evangelie', in G.Quispel (ed.), *Gnosis. De derde component van de Europese cultuurtraditie*, Utrecht 1988, 85–99.
4. Saxer, *Le culte de Marie Madeleine* (n.2), 327; Marina Warner, *Alone of all Her Sex. The Myth and the Cult of the Virgin Mary*, London 1976, 224–35. The belief that Mary the mother of Jesus was born without (original) sin (the Immaculate Conception) grew. The popularity of Mary Magdalene in the Middle Ages and during the Counter-Reformation kept pace with it. Mary, the sinless mother of Jesus, came to be ever further removed from ordinary believers. Mary Magdalene with her sinful past could fill this gap. For a brief survey of the tradition about Mary Magdalene see Paul-Marie Guillaume, 'Marie Madeleine (St)', *Dictionnaire de la Spiritualité*, Paris 1980.
5. Haskins, *Mary Magdalen* (n.2), 98.
6. Marilene Mosco (ed.), *La Maddalena tra Sacro e Profano*, Florence 1986, 43.
7. Haskins, *Mary Magdalen* (n.2), 188–90.
8. *Latijnsch-Nederlandsch Mis- en Vesperboek*, Turnhout 1925.
9. Pius Parsch, *Het jaar des Heren*, Apeldoorn 1941, 446. See also J.A. Jungmann, *Missarum Solemnia. Eine genetische Erklärung der Römischen Messe*, Vienna 1958, 601–2. The Creed is sung on the festivals of Christ, of Mary the mother of Jesus, of the apostles, at All Saints, and at the consecration of a church.

10. Jacobus de Voragine, *Die Legenda Aurea*, Heidelberg 1975, 472.

11. Luise Rinser, *Miriam*, Utrecht 1985; Nikos Kazantzakis, *The Last Temptation of Christ*, London 1979.

12. Haskins, *Mary Magdalen* (n.2), 476 n.46.

13. Stichting Magdala, Postbus 4114, 1620 HC Hoorn, The Netherlands.

14. *Calendarium Romanum Generale*, Rome 1969, 97–8, 131.

15. Haskins, *Mary Magdalen* (n.2), 249–51. Haskins also mentions Calvin, who attacks the thesis ('of popes, monks and other hypocrites') that the sister of Lazarus is the same person as the woman who was a sinner in Luke.

16. Saxer, *Le culte de Marie Madeleine* (n.2), 5.

17. Peter Ketter, *The Magdalene Question*, Milwaukee 1935.

18. Biblical quotations are taken from the Revised Standard Version. Wherever necessary, male terms which do not have an exclusively masculine reference have been made inclusive terms.

19. J.Sickenberger, 'Ist die Magdalenen-Frage wirklich unlösbar?', *Biblische Zeitschrift* 17, 1926, 63–74.

20. U.Holzmeister, 'Die Magdalenenfrage in der kirchlichen Überlieferung', *Zeitschrift für Katholische Theologie* 46, 1922, 402–22, 556–84.

21. O.Wimmer, *Handbuch der Namen und Heiligen. Mit einer Geschichte des christlichen Kalenders*, Munich 1966, 370–1, 550.

22. Eva M.Synek, '"Die andere Maria." Zum Bild der Maria von Magdala in den östlichen Kirchentraditionen', *Oriens Christianus* 79, 1995, 181–96: 187.

23. Haskins, *Mary Magdalen* (n.2), 94–7.

24. Elisabeth Moltmann-Wendel, *The Women around Jesus*, London and New York 1982, 64.

25. Haskins, *Mary Magdalen* (n.2), 96–7.

26. Although Synek, '"Die andere Maria"' (n.22), gives impressive examples of Eastern church fathers who on the basis of Mary Magdalene argue for a greater role of women in the church.

27. Haskins, *Mary Magdalen* (n.2), 397; she gives more examples.

28. Victor Saxer, 'Les origines du culte de Sainte Marie Madeleine en Occident', in *Marie Madeleine dans la mystique, les arts et les lettres*, Paris 1989, 33–47. Mary Magdalene is mentioned in Bede's (died 735) calendar of saints. She appears there without further explanation. Later writers, following the *Libellus apostolorum* of Ado of Vienne (died 875), added: 'From whom as the Gospel reports, the Lord drove out seven demons. Moreover, along with other extraordinary favours, she had the privilege of being the first to see Christ risen from the dead.' For various local usages see Saxer, *Le culte de Marie Madeleine* (n.2).

29. Both Haskins (*Mary Magdalen* [n.2], 249–51) and Warner (*Alone of all Her Sex* [n.4], 234) point out the interest of the Counter-Reformation in preserving Mary Magdalene as a popular penitent in church tradition.
30. Dutch National Council for the Liturgy, *Altaarmissaal voor de Nederlandse kerkprovincie*, 1978, 864.
31. Malvern, *Venus in Sackcloth* (n.2), 13–15, 170–80.

2. The Earliest Sources about Mary Magdalene

1. In Gert J.Peelen, *Opwaarse wegen. Een bloemlezing uit de poëzie der 'jong protestanten' (1923–1940)*, Kampen 1986, 45.
2. Margaret Starbird, *The Woman with the Alabaster Jar. Mary Magdalen and the Holy Grail*, Santa Fé 1993; Michael Baigent, Richard Leigh and Henry Lincoln, *Holy Blood, Holy Grail*, New York 1983.
3. Thus no attention will be paid in this book to later revelations about Mary Magdalene, for instance the revelations of Jesus in Maria Hillen, *Een daad van liefde*, Heemstede 1992, or the visions of the nineteenth-century Anna Katharina Emmerich, in Clemens Brentano, *Leben der heiligen Jungfrau Maria*, Aschaffenburg.
4. For a summary of the discussion see Frédéric Manns, 'Magdala dans les sources littéraires', in *Studia Hierosolymitana. In onore del P. Bellarmino Bagatti. I Studi Archeologici*, Studium Biblicum Franciscanum, Collectio Maior 22, Jerusalem 1976, 307–37, especially 307–20. Manns gives a survey of all the early texts about Magdala-Tarichea.
5. Manns, 'Magdala' (n.4), 335.
6. For a survey see Jack Finegan, *The Archeology of the New Testament: The Life of Jesus and the Beginning of the Early Church*, revised edition, Princeton 1994, 81–3.
7. For the building that could be the larger synagogue see Vergilio Corbo, 'La città Romana di Magdala', *Studia Hierosolymitana* 1, 1976, 358–78, especially 367. Perhaps the question of the inhabitants of Magdala to Resh Lakish (third century) is connected with both discoveries: 'Can one make use of stones from a synagogue that has been destroyed to build another one?' (Megilla 3, 73d).
8. Manns, 'Magdala' (n.4), 320–9.
9. Stanislao Loffreda, 'Magdala – Tarichea', *Bibbia e Oriente* 18, 1976.3–4, 133–5.
10. H.L.Jones, *The Geography of Strabo* I, London 1930, introduction.
11. G.Dalman, *Arbeit und Sitte in Palästina*, V, *Webstoff, Spinnen, Weben, Kleidung*, Gütersloh 1937, 70–1.

12. For a survey see Sean Freyne, *Galilee from Alexander the Great to Hadrian*, Wilmington 1980; W. Bosen, *Galiläa als Lebensraum und Wirkungsfeld Jesu*, Freiburg im Breisgau 1985.

13. Hellmut Gollwitzer and Pinchas Lapide, *Een vluchtelingenkind. Gedachten over Lucas 2*, Baarn 1984, 15–16.

14. Two other arguments for this are that Jesus very probably spoke Aramaic and, as the New Testament Gospels attest, above all addressed the people of Israel.

15. When Karl Rengstorf describes the disciples of a rabbi, as their prime characteristic, after following him, he mentions how they serve him: in G.Kittel et al., *Theological Dictionary of the New Testament 4*, 427–8.

16. It is difficult to say precisely what the position of women in Palestine was in the time of Jesus (for example, how much freedom of movement they had). There is little material about this period. The material that there is is either of a later date, or prescriptive rather than descriptive. There is a tendency to set Jesus' attitude towards women against the dark background of the Jewish attitude of this time. Whether this is correct is questionable. See Elisabeth Schüssler Fiorenza, *In Memory of Her. A Feminist Theological Reconstruction of Christian Origins*, Boston and London 1983, 106–18. She refers to the Jewish book of Judith, which was written in the first century of our era. Judith is a widow who inherits the estate of her husband. A female steward administers this for her. Judith is independent and has great freedom. She can refuse a second marriage. She can devote her life to prayer, asceticism and observing the sabbath. She can criticize the elders of her city for their folly and their theologically perverse judgment. She travels with her maid and without any male escort, and causes no scandal; all this is described with approval.

17. Friedrich Blass, Albert Debrunner and Friedrich Rehkopf, *Grammatik des neutestamentlichen Griechisch*, Göttingen 1990, para.441.

18. For conventional and alternative wisdom, see Marcus Borg, *Jesus. A New Vision. Spirit, Culture and the Life of Discipleship*, San Francisco 1987.

19. This is a possible translation of the verse which does more justice to the Greek word *ego* used here, emphasizing the word 'I' (see Theodor Zahn, *Kommentar zum Neuen Testament. Das Evangelium des Matthäus*, Leipzig 1910, 340). Whether Jesus is expressing his own hesitation or that of the bystanders is not completely clear. Nor is it clear in the case of the woman (Matt.15.21–28). Given Jesus' view of uncleanness one would expect the latter. Luke confirms that hesitation would be the normal reaction. The Jewish

elders indicate that. They, not the centurion himself, come to Jesus with the request and they 'besought him earnestly' with the argument that the centurion 'loves our nation, and he built us our synagogue' (Luke 7.5).

20. See, for example, Eduard Schweizer's reaction to Bernadette Brooten's article: E.Schweizer, 'Scheidungsrecht der jüdischen Frau? Weibliche Jünger Jesu?', *Evangelische Theologie* 42, 1982, 294–300. See also E.P.Sanders, *The Historical Figure of Jesus*, London 1993, 110, who presupposes that the women following Jesus provided homes and food and rarely actually followed Jesus, except for example on the pilgrimage to Jerusalem. His argument for this is that it would not have been the custom for men and women to travel together. Had they done so, we would have heard more in the New Testament about this scandalous behaviour. Sanders does not substantiate his argument. Here he is not alone in his comments on the women disciples. In Chapter 3 we shall see that the third-century church fathers always assume that the female and male disciples travelled together.

21. Schüssler Fiorenza, *In Memory of Her* (n.16), 106–59.

22. For asceticism see the argument of Susanne Heine, *Women and Early Christianity. Are the Feminist Scholars Right?*, London 1987, 65–70; also Matt.19.12.

23. Ulrich B. Müller, 'Vision und Botschaft', *Zeitschrift für Theologie und Kirche* 74, 1977, 416–48, especially 435.

24. See n.13 and also Karl Rengstorf, '*Didasko*', in *Theological Dictionary of the New Testament* (n.15) 2, 156 n.40.

25. Some manuscripts have 'him' instead of 'them'. However, 'them' is usually opted for as the correct reading. See J.A.Fitzmyer, *The Gospel according to Luke. Introduction, Translation and Notes*, New York 1981, 698.

26. Sarah B.Pomeroy, *Goddesses, Whores, Wives and Slaves. Women in Classical Antiquity*, New York 1975, 132, 150–70, see above all 151–2 and 166; David Daube, *The Duty of Procreation*, Edinburgh 1977.

27. In the Jewish tradition, women were not accepted as witnesses: Deut.19.15–17; Sifre Deut 19.17 par.190 (109b); (H.L.Strack and) P.Billerbeck, *Kommentar zum Neuen Testament aus Talmud und Midrasch* III, Munich 1926, 560c; cf. Edward Lynn Bode, *The First Easter Morning. The Gospel Accounts of the Women's Visit to the Tomb of Jesus*, Analecta Biblica 45, Rome 1970, 161. Roman legislation regarded women as weak, insignificant, frivolous and fickle, Pomeroy, *Goddesses, Whores, Wives and Slaves* (n.26), 150.

28. Bode, *The First Easter Morning* (n.27), 161, 173–4, takes the same view.

29. According to Josephus, women and children were also crucified

(*Jewish War* II, 307). According to Luise Schottroff, 'Maria Magdalena und die Frauen am Grabe Jesu', *Evangelische Theologie* 42, 1982, 3–25: 7–8, the tombs of political opponents of the Roman empire were sometimes seen by the authorities as places of possible conspiracy. Anyone who visited such a grave was taking a great risk. See also Raymond E. Brown, 'The Burial of Jesus (Mark 15:42–27)', *The Catholic Biblical Quarterly* 50, 1988, 233–45.

30. Except for John 19.25.

31. For the punctuation see Blass, Debrunner and Rehkopf, *Grammatik des neutestamentlichen Griechisch* (n.17), paras. 386.1; 397.5; 470.1; see also Schottroff, 'Maria Magdalena und die Frauen' (n.29), 20.

32. There is agreement that vv.9–20 were added later. For an account of various views about the original conclusion see Gerald O'Collins, 'The Fearful Silence of Three Women (Mark 16:8c)', *Gregorianum* 69, 1988, 489–503.

33. Schottroff, 'Maria Magdalena und die Frauen' (n.29), 20f.; J.David Hester, 'Dramatic Inconclusion: Irony and the Narrative Rhetoric of the Ending of Mark', *Journal for the Study of the New Testament* 57, 1995, 61–86.

34. Martin Hengel, 'Maria Magdalena und die Frauen als Zeugen', in Otto Betz, *Abraham Unser Vater. Festschrift für Otto Michel*, Leiden 1963, 243–56.

35. F.Neyrinck, 'Les Femmes au Tombeau: Étude de Ia redaction Matthéenne (Mat. XXVIII. 1–10)', *New Testament Studies* 15, 1969, 168–90.

36. See n.31. It is clear in Matthew that only the brethren will see Jesus in Galilee.

37. Karl Rengstorf, in G.Kittel et al., *Theological Dictionary of the New Testament* 2, 623–31.

38. Max Pohlenz, *Stoa. Geschichte einer geistigen Bewegung*, Göttingen 1948, 64–158: 87–8; Kurt Rudolph, *Gnosis* , Edinburgh 1984, 76–7, 98–9. The microcosm is a reflection of the macrocosm. The eight parts of the soul are a reflection of the seven planets and the eighth, divine sphere above them.

39. For a survey of the position of women in Hellenism see Carl Schneider, *Kulturgeschichte des Hellenismus*, Munich 1967, I, 78–117. He concludes: 'Misogyny is a Hellenistic creation' (116). According to Schneider, the sometimes very negative Hellenistic verdict on women is a reaction to the fact that Hellenistic culture offered scope to women. They went with the army, they were professional sportswomen, owned property, were doctors, poetesses, heads of state, philosophers and musicians. Women also came to life more than ever in art (e.g. in the plays of Euripides).

40. Philo, *Questions and Answers on Genesis* II.49 and IV.148.
41. According to the quotation from ibid,, IV.15.
42. See also the Gospel of Thomas, Logion 114.
43. Unless we assume that Luke was referring to them in Acts 13.31, see R.Ryan, 'The Women from Galilee and Discipleship in Luke', *Biblical Theology Bulletin* 15, 1985, 56–9.
44. Exegetes today usually opt for four women. Earlier the interpretation which presupposed three women under the cross was popular. See H.-J.Klauck, 'Die dreifache Maria. Zur Rezeption von Joh 19.25 in EvPhiI 32', in F. van Seebroeck, et al. (eds.), *The Four Gospels 1992. Festschrift Frans Neyrinck*, III, Louvain 1992, 2343–57. Klauck thinks that the possibility of two women is not taken seriously enough and concludes that although there is much to be said for four women, we cannot be certain (2346, 2351).
45. According to modern exegetes the beloved disciple is either Lazarus or John Mark, or John the son of Zebedee, or a symbolic figure. Klauck thinks that by contrast the second-century Gospel of Philip puts forward Mary Magdalene as the beloved disciple of John 19.26 (ibid., 2355–6).
46. Raymond E.Brown, *The Gospel according to John*, New York 1970, 694–5.
47. The Greek word here can also mean 'brothers and sisters'. I adopt this translation because in the Gospel of John women play a clear role as disciples of Jesus. See also Raymond E. Brown, 'Roles of Women in the Fourth Gospel', *Theological Studies* 36, 1975, 688–99.
48. While it is true that John 20.17 cannot be understood without John 13–17 (Jesus' farewell discourses at the Passover meal), here the proclamation is broadened. In 15.15 the disciples are no longer servants of Jesus but friends. Now they are brothers and sisters, together children of the one Father. Those who believe in Jesus and are born of the spirit can become children of God (John 1.12–13; 3.5, cf. 14.26–27). Mary Magdalene is the one who may go to the disciples to tell them that from now on this is possible; see Brown, *The Gospel according to John* (n.46), 1014–17.
49. They are also comparable in another sense. In the various summaries of the male disciples and the women, all four Gospels mention Peter first among the men and Mary Magdalene first among the women: Hengel, 'Maria Magdalena und die Frauen' (n.34), 243–56.
50. There is agreement that John 21, in which Peter is central, is a later addition. The Gospel according to John ends at John 20.31. In contrast to the first three Gospels, in John it is not Peter who recognizes Jesus as the Christ but Martha (John 11.27; cf. Mark 8.27–30/Matt.16.13–20/Luke 9.18–21).

3. *The Search Continued*

1. See W.Schneemelcher and R.McL.Wilson, *New Testament Apocrypha* I, second edition, Louisville and Cambridge 1991, 9–61, especially 31f. There is general agreement that whether or not writings were preserved was the result of a process of growth and not of a firm pronouncement. Here, however, the authority of theologians and bishops must not be underestimated.

2. J.B.Mayor, 'Mary', in James Hastings (ed.), *Dictionary of the Bible*, Edinburgh 1900ff., III, 278b–286a: 278b.

3. Friedrich Hauck, '*Kopos/Kopiao*', in G.Kittel et al., *Theological Dictionary of the New Testament* 3, 827–9.

4. Tertullian, *Against Marcion* IV.9.1.

5. Tertullian, *On Marrying Only Once*, 8.6.

6. Pseudo-Cyprian, *On the Unmarried State of Clergy* 25.

7. Hippolytus, *On the Song of Songs,* XXV, 8.

8. Ibid., XXV, 10.

9. Pseudo-Clement of Rome, *Two Letters on Virginity*, 2.15.

10. Ibid.

11. Hippolytus, *On the Song of Songs,* XXV, 3–6.

12. Hippolytus, *Refutation of all Heresies* V, 7,1. In the text he speaks of Mariamne. It is generally thought that this is a reference to Mary Magdalene.

13. See the Letter of the Apostles (*Epistula Apostolorum*). Here Sarah, Martha and Mary Magdalene are mentioned.

14. Origen, *Against Celsus* V, 62.

15. See also Tertullian, *On the Soul* 25, 8. Tertullian also mentions the seven evil spirits. He does that when he wants to maintain, against Plato, the possibility that two souls of equal substance can come together. Mary Magdalene's soul co-existed with a sevenfold evil spirit.

16. Irenaeus, *Against the Heresies* V, 31, 2, and Dionysius, *Letter to Basilides*, canon 1.

17. Origen, *Commentary on John* VI, 287; X, 245; XIII, 179–180.

18. Origen, *Against Celsus* V, 62.

19. Kathleen Corley, '*Noli me tangere*'. *Mary Magdalene in the Patristic Literature*. To my knowledge, this has not been published. Corley concludes from the many references in the fourth century that towards this time Mary Magdalene had become an accepted figure in Orthodox Christianity.

20. Ambrose, *On the Christian Faith* 4, 2, 25.

21. Jerome, *To Anthony* (Letter 12).

22. Jerome, *To Marcella* (Letter 59).

23. Augustine, *Sermon* 244.2–3.

24. Augustine, *Sermon* 232.2.
25. The usual names for the two church orders are, respectively, *Didascalia Apostolorum* and *Canones ecclesiastici sanctorum Apostolorum*.
26. There is a survey in François Bovon, 'Le privilège Pascal de Marie Madeleine', *New Testament Studies* 30, 1984, 50–62. For a thorough investigation see Anti Marjanen, *The Woman Jesus Loved. Mary Magdalene in the Nag Hammadi Library and Related Documents*, Nag Hammadi and Manichaean Studies 40, Leiden 1996.
27. *Apostolic Church Order* III, 6.
28. *Catholic Teaching of the Holy Apostles*, 26.
29. *Apostolic Church Order* III, 12. For the substance of this function see Roger Gryson, *Le ministère des femmes dans l'église ancienne*, Recherches et synthèses, section d'histoire IV, Gembloux 1972, 75–9.
30. *Apostolic Church Order* V, 14.
31. The Acts of Philip have been handed down to us in very fragmentary form. The quotations are taken from Bovon, 'Le privilège Pascal de Marie Madeleine' (n.26), and refer to the manuscript *Vaticanus graecus 808*.
32. Acts of Philip 185.
33. Of the forty-six questions, Mary Magdalene asks thirty-nine.
34. Gospel of Thomas, Logion 21, and Wisdom of Jesus Christ 114.9–10.
35. Wisdom of Jesus Christ 98.10–11.
36. Dialogue of the Saviour 126, 19–20.
37. Dialogue of the Saviour 139, 20–21.
38. E.g. Pistis Sophia 17–18, 60–62, 112–113.
39. Dialogue of the Saviour 139, 13–14.
40. Pistis Sophia 17.
41. Pistis Sophia 19.
42. Pistis Sophia 25.
43. Pistis Sophia 96.
44. Origen, *Catena of Fragments on I Corinthians*, 74, 2–37; found in R.Roukema, *De uitleg van Paulus' eerste brief aan de Corinthiërs in de tweede en derde eeuw*, Kampen 1996, 218.
45. Pistis Sophia 122. See Gospel of Thomas, Logion 114; found in Pheme Perkins, *The Gnostic Dialogue. The Early Church and the Crisis of Gnosticism*, New York 1980, 140–1.
46. The Letter of the Apostles 10–11.
47. Gospel of Philip 59.6–10.

4. The Gospel of Mary

1. The codex is also denoted by the abbreviation BG (Berolinensis Gnosticus). That makes the Gospel of Mary BG 1. I shall refer to the papyrus as EvMar (Evangelium Mariae). See also M.Tardieu and J.-D.Dubois, *Introduction à la Littérature gnostique, 1: Collections retrouvées avant 1945*, Paris 1986, 97–138.

2. W.C.Till, *Die gnostischen Schriften des koptischen Papyrus Berolinensis 8502*, Texte und Untersuchungen zur Geschichte der altchristlichen Literatur 60, Berlin 1955 (second edition revised by H.-M. Schenke 1972). On pp.1–3 he describes the problems of this first edition.

3. J.M.Robinson, *The Nag Hammadi Library in English*, third completely revised edition, Leiden 1988.

4. A. Pasquier, *L'Evangile selon Marie. Texte établi et présenté*, Bibliothèque Copte de Nag Hammadi, section 'textes' 10, Quebec 1983; G.P.Luttikhuizen, *Gnostische Geschriften 1: Het Evangelie naar Maria, het Evangelie naar Filippus, de Brief van Petrus aan Filipus*, Kampen 1986.

5. C.H.Roberts, *Catalogue of the Greek and Latin Papyri in the John Rylands Library Manchester III. Theological and Literary Texts (Nos.457–551)*, Manchester 1938, 18–23. Roberts arrives at his conclusion on the basis of a comparison with P.Oxy VII.110 and P.Oxy VI.83.

6. R.Wilson, 'The New Testament in the Gospel of Mary', *New Testament Studies* 3, 1956/1957, 236–43.

7. According to G.Quispel, 'Das Hebräerevangelium im gnostischen Evangelium nach Maria', *Vigiliae Christianae* 11, 1957, 139–44, the Gospel of Mary uses the Gospel of the Hebrews from the first half of the second century. The passage in question is EvMar 10.15–16. They could both also be drawing on an earlier source.

8. Verse 33a follows on from v.37 without a break. Verses 33b–36 would have been added around the turn of the century. For extended text-critical arguments and a discussion of the content see Gordon D. Fee, *God's Empowering Presence. The Holy Spirit in the Letters of Paul*, Peabody 1994, 272–81.

9. For female leadership in the early church see Constance F. Parvey, 'The Theology and Leadership of Women in the New Testament', in Rosemary Radford Ruether (ed.), *Religion and Sexism. Images of Woman in the Jewish and Christian Traditions*, New York 1974, 117–49; Elisabeth Schüssler Fiorenza, 'Word, Spirit and Power: Women in Early Christian Communities', in Rosemary Radford Ruether and Eleanor Mclaughlin (eds.), *Female Leadership in the Jewish and Christian Traditions*, New York, 1979, 29–70; ead., *In*

Memory of Her. A Feminist Theological Reconstruction of Christian Origins, Boston and London 1983, esp. 160–241.

10. Till, *Die gnostischen Schriften* (n.2), 7.

11. D. Lührmann, 'Die Griechischen Fragmente des Mariae-evangeliums P.Ox 3525 und P.Ryl 463', *Novum Testamentum* 30, 1988, 321–38.

12. Carl Schneider, *Kulturgeschichte des Hellenismus*, Munich 1967, II, 234f.

13. Bernard P. Grenfell and Arthur S. Hunt, *The Oxyrhynchus Papyri*, London 1898–.

14. Successively Gospel of Thomas, Logion 114; Pistis Sophia, chs. 36 and 72; Gospel of Philip 63.32–64.5.

15. For other translations from the Coptic see Luttikhuizen, *Gnostische Geschriften* 1 (n.4), Pasquier, *L' Evangile selon Marie* (n.4); Tardieu and Dubois, *Introduction à la Littérature gnostique* (n.1); Till, *Die gnostischen Schriften* (n.2); G.W.Macrae, R.McL.Wilson and D.M.Parrott (in *The Nag Hammadi Library*, n.3); and Karen King, 'The Gospel of Mary' (n. 20 below). In the Gospel of Mary the terms 'Son of Man' and 'Man' are non-generic Coptic (Greek) terms. I consulted *An Inclusive Language Lectionary. Readings for Year A*, by the National Council of the Church of Christ in the USA, revised edition, 1986, 10–11 and 173–4. On the basis of this, 'Son of Man' has been translated 'the Human One' and 'Man' has been translated 'Human Being'. See also Denise Y.Y.Dijk, 'De feministische liturgische beweging in de Verenigde Staten van Amerika', in Annemarie Korte (ed.), *Proven van vrouwenstudies theologie*, deel IV, Utrecht 1996, 63–110.

16. Michel Tardieu, *Écrits gnostiques. Codex de Berlin*, Paris 1984.

17. For a survey see Hans Jonas, *The Gnostic Religion*, Boston ²1963; Kurt Rudolph, *Gnosis*, Edinburgh 1984; Elaine Pagels, *The Gnostic Gospels*, New York 1979.

18. Pheme Perkins, *The Gnostic Dialogue. The Early Church and the Crisis of Gnosticism*, New York 1980.

19. Karen L.King, *Images of the Feminine in Gnosticism*, Studies in Antiquity and Christianity, Philadelphia 1988.

20. The Gospel of Mary does not give the name of the first power. On the basis of EvMar 16.5–6, where the second and third figures of the Wrath coincide with the second and third powers, one can suppose that the first power is that of Darkness. For the interpretation that Peter is dominated by the Power Wrath see E.A.de Boer, 'Maria van Magdala en haar Evangelie', in G.Quispel (ed.), *Gnosis. De derde component van de Europese cultuurtraditie*, Utrecht 1988, 97; see also Karen King, 'The Gospel of Mary', in R.J.Miller (ed.), *The Complete Gospels. Annotated Scholars Version*, California 1992, 359.

21. Max Pohlenz, *Die Stoa. Geschichte einer geistigen Bewegung*, Göttingen 1948, 367 and 363–6.
22. Gospel of Thomas, Logion 114 and Eph.4.14. In Ephesians this is the only passage; elsewhere the talk is of human beings.
23. Gnostic literature speaks of the 'immovable race'. Earlier it was thought that this denoted a particular trend, Sethian Gnosticism. M.A. Williams, *The Immovable Race. A Gnostic Designation and the Theme of Stability in Late Antiquity*, Nag Hammadi Studies 29, Leiden 1985, has shown that being immovable is a theme that occurred throughout antiquity.
24. The first view is represented by Aristotle and the second by the Stoic Poseidonius of Apamea. Philo seems to know both views. See Hans Leisegang, *Der heilige Geist. Das Wesen und Werden der mystisch-intuitive Erkenntnis in der Philosophie und Religion der Griechen*, Darmstadt 1967, 176–7.
25. Ibid., 87. See Philo, *Allegorical Interpretation* I, 31–32, 37–38.
26. Ibid., 139–40. For *nous* as father see Philo, *Allegorical Interpretation* II, 51 and III, 84; for *nous* as teacher ibid., III, 50; for *nous* as pilot, ibid, III, 24, and Philo, *That the Worse is Wont to Attack the Better*, 53; for *nous* as origin of the good, Philo, *About the Sacrifices of Abel and Cain*, 54; for *nous* as shepherd, Philo, *About Agriculture* 48, 66; for *nous* as God, Philo, *Allegorical Interpretation* I, 40.
27. See above all the section on Poseidonius of Apamea in Pohlenz, *Die Stoa* (n.21).
28. For examples and background see Ioan Petru Culianu, *Psychanodia I. A survey of the evidence concerning the ascension of the soul and its relevance*, Leiden 1983. He shows that the 'journey of the soul' was a widespread theme in antiquity.
29. See for example *The Exegesis on the Soul* and *Authoritative Teaching* (Nag Hammadi Library II.6 and VI.3). The *Corpus Hermeticum* also knows of the struggle of the soul now. In Tractate XIII the thrice mighty Hermes describes to his son Tat the twelve tribulations that the soul endures – unconsciousness, lack of control, desire, injustice, greed, mendacity, envy, deceit, wrath, a hot temper, malice – and which it can combat with the ten spiritual Powers of the mercy of God. These are the knowledge of God, the experience of joy, self-control, will-power, righteousness, generosity, truthfulness, happiness, light and life. With God's help the struggle is fought in this life and issues in rebirth. Hermes says: 'He who through God's mercy has gained a part in birth from God has left sensual perception behind him: he knows himself, he knows that he is formed by the spiritual powers and he feels joy in his heart' (*Corpus Hermeticum* XIII, 10). After death there is another

journey of the soul which is no longer a fight, but a surrender of the functions which belong to the body. See *Corpus Hermeticum, translated into Dutch with an introduction and commentary* by R. van den Broek and G.Quispel, Amsterdam 1991.

30. The use of the word 'rest' does not offer any help either. Eternal rest is to be found only with God, but rest can already be experienced now as a gift of grace, see Jan Helderman, *Die Anapausis im Evangelium Veritatis. Eine vergleichende Untersuchung des valentinianisch-gnostischen Heilsgutes der Ruhe im Evangelium Veritatis und in anderen Schriften der Nag Hammadi-Bibliothek,* Nag Hammadi Studies 18, Leiden 1984. This notion appears not only in Gnosticism but also outside it, e.g. in Philo. In his work *On Dreams* (1.112–113), Philo uses the words 'rest in silence' (cf. EvMar 17.4–7) for the here and now when through the help of God thought frees the soul from the domination of sensual perception. See Helderman, 59 and 80 n.119. Philo describes this 'resting in silence' as an experience of comfort.

31. As for the Gospel according to Mary, H.Koester and J.M.Robinson, *Trajectories through Early Christianity,* Philadelphia 1971, think that the Gnostic dialogue developed from the same material as the genre of the Gospel and that in it New Testament material was unconsciously transformed. The Gnostic dialogue would be the last development of the genre of revelation Gospel which gives a central place to thoughts about the future and the heavenly reality which can already be experienced now. It expresses the earliest confession, 'Jesus is Lord'. The titles Lord and Son of Man are used to indicate this.

32. The standpoints of Perkins and Pagels respectively, see Perkins, *The Gnostic Dialogue* (n.18), 136 n.10.

33. See C.Schmidt, *Pistis Sophia. Ein gnostisches Originalwerk,* Leipzig 1925, LXXXVII–III. He writes: 'Here in my view we have the germ from which the later high esteem of Mary Magdalene developed or was handed down.'

34. See e.g. Perkins, *The Gnostic Dialogue* (n.18), 136–7, 141.

35. See Chapter 2 n.26.

36. Capernaum had a very big synagogue. A Roman garrison was stationed there. Excavations there have uncovered 'miserable huts', see Chapter 2, n. 9. Women had less freedom of movement in a Jewish environment than in more Hellenistic surroundings.

5. *Mary Magdalene*

1. Susan Haskins, *Mary Magdalen. Myth and Metaphor,* London 1993, 107.

2. R.-G.Coquin and G.Godron, 'Un encomion Copte sur Marie-Madeleine attribué à Cyrille de Jérusalem', *Bulletin de l'Institut Français d'Archéologie Orientale* 90, Cairo 1990. This contains the first publication of this curious document, which has only been preserved in very fragmentary form. Coquin and Godron do not investigate the discovery and the original dating of the Greek original. The writing itself refers to Cyril of Jerusalem. That should mean that it comes from the fourth century. However, a comparable text about Mary the mother of Jesus is attributed to Pseudo-Cyril, see J.Quasten, *Patrology,* III, on Cyril.

3. C.Methuen, 'Widows, Bishops and the Struggle for Authority in the Didascalia Apostolorum', *Journal of Ecclesiastical History* 1995, 197–213. Tertullian reports that women in fact appealed to women before them when he forbids women to baptize and give instruction. They refer to Thecla from the Acts of Paul and Thecla. Tertullian refers them back to the letters of Paul, in which women are commanded to keep silent (Tertullian, *On Baptism* 17.5). See also Eva M.Synek, ' "Die andere Maria." Zum Bild der Maria von Magdala in den östlichen Kirchentraditionen', *Oriens Christianus* 79, 1995, 189–90. Synek demonstrates that the argument was still being used in the twelfth century, but the other way round. The Byzantine Theophanes Kerameus interprets the Thecla tradition as valid alongside Paul's prohibition of women teaching, which was added later. Paul himself had sent out Thecla, his disciple, to teach and proclaim. So how could he have issued a prohibition against teaching?

4. Dialogue of the Saviour 144–6.

Index of Ancient Texts

Bible

Old Testament

New Testament

Gospel of Mary